EVERYTHING'S OKAY

Alesia Shute

Everything's Okay

By Alesia Shute

ISBN: 978-0-9822206-4-1
Library of Congress Control Number: 2009929665

Published by Escalation Press
1670 Valencia Way, Mundelein, IL 60060
Phone: 815.346.2398
email: info@writersoftheroundtable.com

Cover Design by Nathan Brown, Writers of the Round Table Inc.
Layout by Sunny B. DiMartino, www.sunnydimartino.com

Dedication

I dedicate this book to my mother Evelyn and my grandmother Nessie, both of whom were taken from me (us) too early. Sometimes, things happen in life that are beyond our control. My mother was a strength for me, and I know she has watched over me during this entire writing process. Without her influence throughout my life, I would not have become the person I am. I am past being bitter about these two losses in my life and now think of them as positive forces that have driven me to complete this challenge of writing a book.

Acknowledgments

First and foremost I would like to thank my husband Cliff for his patience and support through this entire process. I cannot remember a time when he did not support a project that I wanted to conquer.

I would also like to thank my son and his optimism, which inspired me to finish writing, along with my immediate family and friends who were all so patient while listening to my ideas (whether they wanted to or not!).

Thank you to my sister who has always shown a unique interest in my sickness, something that never came into question while growing up since there was no time to ponder, only to move forward. And thanks to my parents for doing the best possible job they could under the circumstances they were faced with.

Special thanks to Corey Blake and Eva Travers for their encouragement. You helped me in making these words entirely my own.

Thank you to Dr. C Everett Koop and Dr. John Templeton: you both saved my life. In thanks, all of the profits from *Everything's Okay* will be donated to The Children's Hospital of Philadelphia.

My Reflection

When I look back over all the things I've been through in my life, I often think of them as a dream. I think of myself as the little girl I was, and it's as if she is just a thought to me and not the "me" I know at all. I have removed myself from her as if she was another person.

As an adult, I have been able to reflect on this writing process, understanding that my way of thinking was a survival tactic. You will see as my story unfolds that in order for me to get through all of the moments, days, and weeks of my early years, it was easier to stand outside of myself as an observer than it was to be myself. What I could not accept, until now, was that the little girl I have spoken about was really me. For the first time, I can speak of her as "ME" and not as someone else.

I sometimes think of what my life would have been like if I had not been sick and, after a moment, I realize that my challenges were my gift from a higher power. I believe that a path is laid out for all of us from birth, and to some degree, we follow this path. We each encounter circumstances beyond our control and there is a reason for everything that happens. Although we cannot always readily see the reason, some of us will choose to dig deep enough to make some sense of it. This path, chosen for me, created and molded me into the woman I am now: confident, happy, giving, and kind. I do not think that my higher power intentionally made me suffer. The suffering itself falls into the realm of circumstances beyond my control. It's what I learned in the suffering that has made me who I am every step of the way. For that, I must thank whoever set me on this journey.

This writing process has been both challenging and healing, helping me understand what is truly important in life and what is not. The strength I have gained from revisiting and reclaiming my life makes me feel wonderful every day. I am here to share this story with you.

We all have joy and tragedy, pain and sadness, and each of us must choose to either be a victim or not. My choice from a very early age was to be productive in my life—not to play the victim. I have always wanted to feel empowered in all that I do...to make conscious decisions about the kind of person I want to be. Living this way reflects, as you will see, in everything that I do.

I hope you enjoy reading this gathering of my memories and thoughts, and I look forward to continuing this path for as long as possible. If there is any way that I can help you on your path, I hope you will contact me.

—Alesia Shute

CHAPTER 1

MY FIRST LOVE

...I always tried to treat other people with any kind of differences as equal to myself, but now, I was the one who could be rejected.

When I was about 15 years old, I met my first real "love"—or so I thought. His name was Nick, and he was an 18-year-old, tall, dark, Italian guy. I was smitten at first glance. He was really easy to get along with and always made me laugh; our personalities clicked right away. He was one of those people that made me feel comfortable right off the bat. His smile was warm and told me just by looking at him that life was okay, and that there was no reason to get nervous or uptight about anything. He made conversation easily and seemed to get along with everyone. Nick had a small gaming business at a place called Brigantine Castle on a pier in Brigantine, New Jersey, with family-oriented games and prizes. The entire pier, extending out from the boardwalk, was a string of games and restaurants. You couldn't reach any of them without entering first through the Haunted Castle, where I worked when I met Nick.

Nick came from a family that was steeped in the restaurant and gaming business, but his position with the company was still pretty impressive for such a young guy. He hired me after I left my job as a ghoul in the Haunted Castle. I could not stand the ghoul job for too long; I spent too many hours sitting in an empty picture frame, scaring people with fangs hanging out of my mouth. After Nick hired me to run one of the carnival games, we enjoyed each other's company enough to go out. It became serious pretty quickly, and I then realized that I liked him more than anyone I had ever met.

Nick and I spent all of our time together and when we were not together, I thought about him all too often. We went out to dinner and hung out as much as possible, and he got along with my parents and family immediately. He could make me laugh easily and charm me with his easy smile and mannerisms. At that time, he was the most mature guy I had ever met and dated. We were together for about a year, and then one day I got into a deep conversation with my best girlfriend, Randee.

"I really think he may be the one," I said one night while we watched television in her house. Randee looked at me, and we both giggled about what we were thinking: the 'sex thing.'

"Do you really think that this is it and you're ready to 'go' for it?"

"Yes, but what if he thinks I am weird with this 'bag' hanging from my side?"

"Well, if he does act strange after you tell him, he is not the one, right?" Not long after our little conversation, Nick and I got together, and I began to do something I had never had to do before: explain that I am different. I don't really recall where we were at the time, but it must have been his apartment.

"Nick, I need to explain to you about some surgery I have had over the years. I am different than most other girls you have dated." I could feel my heart pounding through my shirt, and a drop of sweat trickled between my breasts. I was trembling slightly and my mouth was a bit dry, but I was determined to explain myself. I was different and needed to accept it whatever the consequences. I never really thought about people not wanting to be around me until that moment.

Throughout my life, I always tried to treat other people with any kind of differences as equal to myself, but now, I was the one who could be rejected. I had an uneasy feeling deep inside that made my head feel a bit funny and my palms sweat. *What if he dumps me,* was all that filled my head for those few moments before we spoke. I managed to suppress this feeling and just plug along, stay brave, and see what the outcome would be. Either way, I could not change myself. This was who I was, what I was. So there I stood, planted to the ground, and continued.

I explained about the "bag," what it was for and why I had it, and he listened very, very carefully. "I have had many surgeries in my short life, and as a sick child, my parents had no choice whether to have this done or not," I continued, telling him that it was a matter of life or death at the point they made this decision. He listened intently. "That is where the 'bag' comes from," I tried to explain. "I will go to the bathroom into this appliance on my side forever. It is a bit strange, something I have grown used to, but it does make me different."

Nick was looking at me with a little sadness and a bit of curiosity, so I decided that this was a great time to continue. "I really felt I needed to tell you this because I think I love you and cannot stop thinking about 'stuff'— wanting to move forward in our relationship." I felt like I was dying inside because I was so scared to be saying this aloud. I did not actually mention having sex with him, but he seemed to know where the conversation was headed.

"You know how much I care for you, Alesia, and if it does not bother you, then it does not bother me," was all that Nick said. It was all he needed to say.

At that moment, I knew that I really was in love with him and I had made the right decision for such a young girl. Here I was, overly worried that I would be rejected when things were going in such a wonderful direction.

After that, we were able to move on in our relationship, and we stayed together for another year. Then we remained on and off for another 6–8 months before we ended the relationship, but I was so very lucky to have had a good "first" experience, both because of my differences and my first choice of sexual partners.

That experience was so positive that with anyone I dated after that, I told them about my sicknesses and the surgeries as if it was no big deal. My positive attitude made others around me feel the same way about me. Not one time can I recall being treated differently.

CHAPTER 2

7 YEARS OLD AND MY WORLD IS CHANGING

Inside the room, I hopped up on the table as I usually did,
swung my feet back and forth, and waited like a good little girl.

I leaned forward with one arm holding my belly, the other arm straight out against the worn out cabinet. My screams were so shrill that I could barely sit up and was forced to remain doubled over in pain until my mother arrived. That was the day that my world changed forever.

Somehow through my screams, I managed to hear my mother coming down the hallway. She came into the small bathroom. She was such a large woman, the room seemed to grow smaller as I watched her walk towards me. She leaned over me and hesitated, looking from my face to the pool of blood beneath me on the floor.

"You must have begun menstruating," she said as she knelt down next to me in the bathroom. I looked at her, not quite able to understand what menstruating was at such a young age. I continued to cry out in pain. She seemed to be thinking out loud at that moment. "I think you are way too young for this. Girls usually do not get their period until they are teenagers," she told me. It was around 1969. I would have been 7 years old. After she helped me clean myself up, she quickly called our medical doctor.

The very next day we headed to our family doctor. I was still very upset from the incident in the bathroom the day before as my mother parked the car. I slowly opened the car door and headed up the three or four steps into

4

the waiting area of the doctor's office. As I sat down and looked around the small waiting room, I got scared thinking I might have to get a needle. Mom checked in, and when she walked away from me, I felt sick inside and confused about what was about to happen to me. How was the doctor going to find out why I was bleeding and in such pain?

When the nurses called my name, I got up slowly, grabbed my mother's hand and walked down the narrow hallway to the examination room on the right. Inside the room, I hopped up on the table as I usually did, swung my feet back and forth, and waited like a good little girl. Dr. McGlocklin walked in with his stethoscope around his neck and smiled at me as usual. He spoke to my mother a bit so she could explain exactly what had happened. Then he turned toward me and began to ask me a few questions.

"Alesia, are you in pain now?" he began. I shook my head no and he continued. "From what your mom tells me, I think I need to examine you a little bit further. Lie down on your side and Mom will help you remove your panties for me. I need you to lie still and hold Mom's hand so that I can get a good look at you and see what is going on to make your tummy hurt so much, okay?" he said.

He then probed me with some kind of scope that had a light. My scream was loud enough that I imagined the other children in the waiting room curled up in their mother's laps, terrified by the sound of fear coming from the examining room.

"Lisa (the name my family called me), calm down, hold my hand and try to lie still," my mother said with tears in her eyes as I lay there on my side, and she leaned down to meet me face to face.

"It will be over very soon and the doctor needs to do this to find out why you are having such bad pain." Her voice was soft and tender, and she held my hand and stared straight into my eyes while I cried and screamed.

The scope looked kind of like a gun with a small light on it. When he inserted it into my rectum, I felt as if I was being torn apart. The exam was only a few minutes, but felt like forever. After the doctor completed the exam, he spoke directly to my mother in a very serious voice. "She needs to see a specialist immediately."

"How can that be?" my mother asked him quietly, trying to protect me from the conversation.

"From what I can tell, she needs more intensive examinations."

That was all he said.

CHAPTER 3

ANOTHER DOCTOR

The pain became part of life. The doctors were a revolving door for me, and the medications were part of waking each morning.

Within days, we were sitting in a specialist's office, waiting for another exam. I was so scared from the last examination that I could not stop trembling. I felt like I would die if anyone did that to me again. My older brother and younger sister went with my mom, dad, and me for the appointment because there was not anyone around to watch them. They began to fight in the waiting room and were quickly reprimanded by my father to behave and be quiet. "Play nice while Mom and I take your sister to meet this doctor," my father said sternly.

"Mom," I began to cry, as we sat together in the specialist's office. "Please do not let them hurt me again, please," I begged her. "I will do anything if you don't let the new doctor touch me, pleeeeaaasssseee!"

Mom did not have much to say. "Lisa, we have to do this. You have to do this. I will be there to hold you, and it will be over before you know it," she told me. I knew she was lying, but I also knew she was right and that I had to listen to what she told me to do.

My name was called, and off my mother and I went down the hall to the examination room where we waited to meet the doctor. Inside the room was a long table with lots of stuff scattered around and big lights. I could only imagine what some of the instruments were for, but I really did not want to know. I wanted to go home, play with my baby dolls, and dress up in my princess costumes.

"Hello, my name is Dr. Tylor," said this tall man with dark hair. I began to tear up and hide behind my mother. "I understand that your Dr. McGlocklin took a look at you and needs me to examine you so we can tell your mom what we think is wrong."

I began to shake and cry quietly but listened as he continued. "Let's get you undressed and Mom can keep you company. We will do this as quickly as possible so you can go home," he told me. "I want you to understand that I am really trying to help you, but I need you to listen to what I tell you and keep very, very still.

The nurse laid me face down on the table. My mother was allowed to stay in the room with me since I was so very young, and the doctor came in and turned the lights down. "This will hurt you, but I need you to lie as still as possible so that I can see everything clearly," he said. My mother was at the head of the table holding my hand. I began to cry before he even came close. The table began to tilt with my head facing down. He turned on a bright lamp and began to insert a long stick of some sort inside of me. The stick had a light so he could see into my rectum. I held on so tightly to my mother's hand that I was surprised I did not break it off. I began to sob harder, losing control. I did lie still as I was told but began screaming that he had to stop! The pain was more than I could handle. It seemed like forever.

"Please, stop! I think you are going to take out my brain! Please stop!"

I have never experienced anything else quite like this exam. That is the day I think I leapt from being a normal 7-year-old to becoming an adult in a matter of seconds. I started to detach myself from the pain...a survival technique.

Up to that point, I really was only in the beginning phases of what I was about to experience. I went numb somehow and just began to go through the motions. The pain became part of life. The doctors were a revolving door for me, and the medications were part of waking each morning. My entire family began to absorb what I was going through, and without any of us realizing it, all of our lives began to change. Every plan for every day would dangle relative to how sick or weak I was, or how many appointments I had.

We all became sick—not just me. My siblings suffered in different ways than I, but we all suffered. And the level of maturity I reached by age 10 was staggering. Those were the cards I was dealt.

I began to look at myself as one person and at the sick child as someone else.

CHAPTER 4

A DIAGNOSIS

*"I pray that God will make me okay," I said quietly under the covers
of my hospital bed that night. "How could a little girl really die—
just like that?"*

I was immediately swept off to Nazareth Hospital in Northeast Philadelphia for a week and was then transferred to Jefferson Hospital in Center
City Philadelphia. At Jefferson, I shared a ward with many other children
that I thought were much sicker than I was. One young girl, Michelle, was
3 or 4 years old. She had swallowed cleaning products from under her mother's kitchen sink and had to eat through a feeding tube in her nose as a result.
The products burned out her esophagus and she could not eat or drink anything normally. At mealtime, she would still sit with us, chew her food, and
then spit it back out onto the tray. Amazing how she understood that she
could not swallow.

One late night, as I lay in my bed, I could hear the nurse speaking softly
in the hall. I looked up to see nurses taking the child in the next room out
with a sheet draped over her. I was in my bed watching through the half
opened door. After they removed the child, a nurse with a pretty white
nurse's hat came into my room to speak to me. She explained to me that "the
little girl was so sick that she had to be taken to heaven. The doctors tried to
help her but could not and only God could make her feel better now." I was
so scared after she told me this that I felt sick and was scared to go to sleep.

"I pray that God will make me okay," I said quietly under the covers of
my hospital bed that night. "How could a little girl really die—just like that?"

10

I whispered to myself as if in a prayer. I now understood that we could die anytime. I was frightened by the image of the girl under the sheet and tried to bury that fear. I never spoke about it to my parents.

The hallways were so very quiet, and I vaguely remember how they tried to shield us from the tragedy. I worried for others even as sick and as young as I was. I lay in my bed that night thinking of how I may have been able to help this child. I have no idea what I could have done, but I felt the strong urge to be there.

After several days in the hospital and a battery of tests, the doctor met with my parents and me again. "Your daughter has something called ulcerative colitis," the doctor at Jefferson told my parents. "She will need many different medications and monitoring throughout this ordeal. This is something you and your family will have to learn to deal with over time," he explained to both my parents.

"What exactly are you trying to tell us?" my mother asked first. "Your diagnosis may well have been in Chinese."

"Is she going to recover? What do we have to do for her?" my father asked. "In layman's terms, what is this colitis thing?"

"Ulcerative colitis is cancer of the large intestine and colon," the doctors explained to my mother and father. Her future is uncertain, but we will begin treating her with a series of medications and diet restrictions in order to get the disease under control. She is extremely young to have developed this disease, and we are puzzled by that at this point. We suggest sending you to the finest doctors available since she is still at such a young age."

For the next few years, until I was about 10, I spent more time in hospitals than out. My final destination was The Children's Hospital of Philadelphia, about a 40-minute ride for my parents. Having to make this commute every day became tedious. What I did not realize was that we were blessed to have such a wonderful hospital, just for children, so close to our home. While there, I met Dr. C. Everett Koop, and again my destiny changed.

Chapter 5

FAMILY LIFE WENT ON

Because I wanted to be normal like all of my friends, I persevered and ignored things that did not agree with me or go my way.

When I was home from the hospital, my life was anything but what I truly wanted. I awoke every morning to breakfast and dozens of pills. I would cry through every swallow. I do not even know how many I took daily, but it seemed like piles.

"Try to eat something and take your pills," Mom would say to me every morning. I knew what I had to do but would cry or find a reason not to do it right away.

"Do I have to?" was always my answer. "Why do I have to do this?"

Then lunchtime would come with the same ritual, as would dinner. My sister and brother would make fun of me because I had so much medicine to take. We were normal siblings, taunting each other, but they had more stuff to taunt me with. After each meal, when everyone was done and Mom was doing the dishes, I was still sitting there, not wanting to eat and not wanting to take the pills. My dad would often sit with me and coax me to finish, sometimes into the evening. My brother and sister just seemed to accept life was this way, as well. All of this became our routine.

I hated to eat and couldn't bring myself to do it. I had to see a therapist through all of this, and the doctors and my parents even tried to use therapy as an angle to get me to eat. Accompanying me on every session was a sandwich that I refused to touch. There was always the same discussion. "Why will you not eat this sandwich?" Dr. Goldman asked me.

"I do not want to have stomach pains anymore," was always my answer.

"Do the pains go away when you do not eat?"

"Not all the way," I had to admit, but any relief was better than none.

Other children were cruel and began to make fun of me because I was so sick, weak, and frail from a huge amount of weight loss. When I had bathroom accidents in the classroom, they snickered and called me "baby." Outside, I could not keep up with the games they played because I was too weak to run. I could not run or jump rope, but I continued to try.

I was determined to be like everyone else. Because I was not shy, I was able to make friends easily, so I did try to keep up with them when we were playing. Often I needed to sit down and watch. I would make up a story that I did not feel like doing something instead of admitting I could not. My teachers allowed me to leave the classroom when I needed to without permission because when the pains began in my stomach, I had to go to the bathroom immediately. If the teacher did not notice my hand raised, I might not make it to the little girl's room.

My first time back at school after a long absence, I began feeling a small bellyache. I quietly slipped out of the classroom and ran to the girl's room. I prayed that no one would be in the hall. Moving as fast as my legs would take me, I lost control of my bowels. Feces was streaming down my legs. As humiliated as I was, I went to the nurse's office.

"Can I call my mother to bring me clothing?" I cried.

She was a nice lady who always understood. "Go into my bathroom and clean yourself up," she said in a very calm voice. "Here, wipe your eyes and I will call your mother."

They helped me change and sent me back to class. The only problem was that I had on another outfit so the few kids that wanted to be mean to me made sure that everyone was aware of my clothing change and that I "must be a baby who should wear diapers." Time and time again, this scene played out, leaving me utterly humiliated. I cried to the nurse almost daily until they finally decided to let me keep an extra set of clothing at the nurse station.

Years later, my mother told me that the teachers had threatened my classmates to keep quiet and not make fun of me. The first few times they made fun of me to my face, I ignored them and walked away. I must have been making believe that I did not hear them because when my mother told me this had happened, I really was very shocked. I do recall some of the negative comments but had let them roll off my back. Because I wanted to be normal like all of my friends, I persevered and ignored things that did not agree with me or go my way. I just blocked them out and moved on with my day-to-day activities as best as I could.

CHAPTER 6

MY NORMAL

"I want to be like everyone else," I told her during one of our arguments, but the reality was that I was frail.

"What do you think you are doing, Lisa?" my mother asked when she spotted me through the kitchen window one day, dragging my bike up the driveway.

"I'll be careful," was my usual answer. I said this without looking up at her so that she wouldn't realize that I was afraid to do physical things. "I want to be like everyone else," I told her during one of our arguments, but the reality was that I was frail. "I know you're right, but I need to start somewhere," I cried to her almost daily. I was determined to run and play like the other kids.

"Be careful, don't overdo it," she yelled out to me as I was off to try something else. She tried to let me be a kid. I considered myself non-athletic. I didn't play any sports in school, partly because they weren't offered to girls in the late 1960s and partly because I simply wasn't very interested. "I want to bake in my Easy Bake Oven and play Barbies," I told myself repeatedly. Truth was, while part of me felt like I *should* be roller-skating, bike riding, and skateboarding, I *preferred* so-called "girly things," and it probably had nothing to do with my illness. Still, part of me felt I had to live up to my friends' expectations. Going out to play on someone's swings was an effort for me, though.

When I grew older, in my middle teens, I dated, went to dances, and hung out with my gang of friends. Weekends consisted of the roller rink, going out for pizza or burgers, and babysitting for extra shopping money. My father went along with my mother's and my decisions. It was partly because he was too busy working and paying all the bills to fight with me about much.

One day it seemed everyone I knew was going off to summer camp. "I want to go to camp and sleep there and have fun and make friends!" I cried to my parents. "Please let me go… I'll be fine… I'm okay," I tried to convince them. Going to overnight camp like my big brother was so important to me, and finally they gave in, although I was a bit young— maybe 8 or 9. So there we were, packing me up for a three-week experience (against my parents' better judgment), but I was convincing.

The ride was so exciting that I barely realized it was nearly three hours long. Finally there, my parents stepped out of the car to unload my suitcases. I was bubbling over with excitement, and they were uncertain as to whether or not they were doing the right thing. Mom took me by the arm and whispered into my ear, "Lisa, you can still change your mind if you want. We can turn around and go home if you do not want to stay."

I felt a bit scared about them leaving me but looked around the camp, smiled, and said, "Mom, I can do this. I want to stay."

Dad helped me to my bunk, bunk number one, and gave me a small hug. "You take care and have some fun, okay?" I walked them to the doorway and kissed them both goodbye. I told them I loved them and that I would write every day.

As the car drove away, I took in my surroundings. It was so pretty with all of the trees. There were bunks that to me looked like little one-floor houses. Eight of them were on the girls' side of the camp. I was told that the boys' side had the same amount of bunks.

There was a big lake, pools, all kinds of activities for us to do, a big cafeteria, and an outdoor theatre. Wow! I was so lucky! When it was time to meet my counselors and fellow campers, I followed one counselor to the main part of the camp where everyone else was and we were placed into groups. Next thing I knew, we were headed back to the bunks to unpack and learn our way around.

I bunked with 10 other girls around my age. We each had a bed, a cubby, and a little chest of drawers. A row of bathrooms connected bunk one, our bunk, and bunk two. Off the bathrooms was a row of showers. I peeked in and saw that there were no curtains—it was one big shower for all of us in the two bunks to share.

We met our counselors—who turned out to be a group of teenage girls—and instantly fell in love with them. They were great to us and seemed cool and easy to get to know. Michele was my favorite. For some reason, she and I instantly bonded, and I began to follow her everywhere.

After a few days of arts and crafts, swimming, and sports, the pain returned. I did not care for any of the food there, and that made me feel even worse because I was already struggling with eating. I suddenly felt homesick, and crying became a daily routine for me. The excitement had worn off and the reality set in—I was ill, I was homesick, and I really missed my mom. I wanted to go home. It had only been a few days, and I was supposed to be there for three weeks. What was I going to do?

The counselors did a great job of helping us forget about missing our moms. "You will be fine in a few days," said Michele. "I promise. All you have to do is relax and participate in the activities that are here for everyone."

I went to Michele often and cried to her about how I missed my mom and needed to go home. Michelle always had a big smile on her face. She had beautiful long, brown hair and looked like a model to me. She grabbed me by the hand, took me to my bed, sat with me, and told me not to worry. "Alesia, don't be so sad," she said. "Everyone feels a little sad. Even I miss my mother, but there is so much to do here. If you try to have fun, before you know it, it will be time to go home. And by then you may even want to stay."

"No," I cried, "I really need to go home! I hate it here. Please call my mom to come and get me, please!" I cried on and off throughout the day.

I even cried when they bribed me with my favorite snack—peanut chews—before the evening shows. I should not have eaten nuts because of my sickness—I wasn't able to digest them—so the pain worsened.

"You can be in the show," the other counselors decided. "Every kid wants to be in the show, but only the special ones get picked."

I cried harder and begged to call home, but they continued trying to

17

distract me.

One night, I woke up another counselor. "Tracy, please help me! I am in such pain, and I need someone to be with me in the bathroom." As she got out of bed, I had an accident all over the floor in the bunk. Luckily, everyone else was asleep, or so I thought.

Tracy got out of bed and took me to the showers. I was a mess. All my clothing was soiled, and I was trembling and crying softly so no one could hear me. She put me in the shower, rinsed my bedclothes, and then cleaned the floor in the bunk. She was only about 17 or 18 years old, but she handled herself so calmly in front of me to avoid upsetting me. Back to bed we went, and I rested well the rest of the night.

The next day, things began to get worse. It turned out one of my bunkmates, Elizabeth, was awake during my ordeal the night before. She told all the other girls what had happened, continued to make fun of me, and would not leave me alone. I could not stop crying after that.

A few days later, the counselors got together, took me into the main office, and called my parents. They sat me in a big chair and told me they were going to call my mother to come and get me. "We accepted your daughter as a camper knowing she is quite ill, and we have tried to give her a wonderful experience, but she is too sick and very unhappy and really needs to go home."

I was relieved to finally be leaving. Even though I tried to love the camp because I wanted to be grown up and do normal "kid" things, I just needed to be home...at least for now. I thought that maybe someday I would try camp again. It could have been a very fun place.

I remained sad throughout the evening show. But afterwards, the counselors pulled me aside and gave me some special treats that they had stashed. It made me feel a little better to be with the older girls alone. "Your parents will be here in the morning," Michele said. "We all want to say goodbye and to let you know that we will miss you." I was so happy that I could not even sleep that night.

The next morning, my parents arrived to take me home. I never went back to camp after that and only made it for 9 days out of 21, but I did it and was satisfied. I practically cried with joy all the way home that day.

CHAPTER 7

NOSE TO NOSE

❦

I could not believe my ears. A dog? I loved dogs!

We were in therapy, just my parents and I this time. The doctor was speaking with my parents about a good way to take the therapy home with us. "She needs a friend, a companion, like a pet of some sort," he told them. "A dog is a good form of therapy for most people. We have seen significant results in some of our patients just by adding a pet to the household."

"Having a pet would be a wonderful gift to keep her company when she feels ill," my mother agreed. I could not believe my ears. A dog? I loved dogs! They always told us "no dogs," but now I heard them agreeing to get one. I sat there with a big smile on my face. They all turned to look at me and my mom asked, "What do you think about getting a dog?"

I'm sure my look said it all, but I spoke up, anyway. "I would love to have a dog! I promise to help take care of it, too!"

I soon learned that nothing felt nicer than to be loved by my dog. That kind of love was unconditional and non-judgmental. Making that decision was probably one of the best things my parents could have done for me. I loved animals so much, and we were a perfect match from the moment we met.

Beepo, a beagle about 6 months old, came to us with her name and we decided to keep it. She came from a family who could not care for her, and they needed to find a good home immediately. My parents were friends with this family so it worked out for everyone when we gave Beepo a new home.

We spent all of our time together, and I tried to teach her a few tricks. "Give me your paw and lie down, Beepo." My mother must have heard me repeat that command about three hours a day. All of us worked with her so much, but she just could not get it. Either she was plain dumb, or we were not very good teachers, but she was still so lovable that I could not be mad at her.

Because I was so proud of my dog, I convinced my mother to let me place her in a local dog show in a nearby park.

"I know I can get her to do whatever I need to win a prize," I told my parents. Not wanting to disappoint me, they agreed after a bit of coaxing on my part, and off we went to Burlhome Park to show off our stuff. When we arrived at the park, I immediately found out how to enter her into different categories. I signed her up for only two events, basic walking and heeling, and favorite tricks. Throughout the entire day, when I entered Beepo in different events, she was unable to live up to the standards of the show. She rolled over when I asked for her paw. When I asked her to lie down, she gave me her paw. She was just as nervous as I was. We did not win anything that day. At the end of it all, I lifted her up onto an empty table and held her face in my hands. I placed my face nose to nose with hers and told her, "I still love you no matter what, Beepo. You may not be a show dog, but you are my baby."

At precisely that moment, a newspaper photographer was passing by and snapped a candid shot of that special moment with my dog. Our picture appeared in the paper, explaining the disappointment we both shared not to win a ribbon. For that, I was totally satisfied with my day. I felt famous.

CHAPTER 8

SICKER AND SICKER

*The counselor and the doctors wanted us to understand
that one sick family member means that the entire family is sick.
We all suffered in different ways.*

Once again, my health began to fail. We went on a series of trips to The
Children's Hospital of Philadelphia, where I began to spend most of
my time either having tests done or being admitted as a patient. I was expe-
riencing dangerous weight loss, and it became clear that the medications
were not working. The cancer was getting worse and spreading through my
intestinal tract. The blood work and barium x-rays revealed that I needed
more intense treatment.

At some point during my testing and doctor visits, I decided to stop
eating. My logic was quite simple for someone so very young: don't eat and
the pain will go away. Kind of smart for an 8-year-old, but of course it didn't
work. My parents began to watch the disease slowly kill me. They also
watched me unintentionally killing myself.

I was suffering so badly with pain and losing weight that at 9 years old,
I only weighed 40 pounds. My newest specialist, Dr. Rosenberg, was a wonderful, kind woman with graying hair who was probably only in her late 40s.
We visited her weekly and went for tests on my intestinal tract that polluted
my body with drugs. I am surprised I survived the treatments—every kind
of x-ray you can imagine.

While in the waiting room at the hospital, my mother sat watching as I
forced down the barium drink. The taste was chalky and made me want to

vomit. "I can't do this!" I cried to her, but she sat calmly and watched until I was finished. Then I was taken into the x-ray room. "Lie down and relax," the nurse told me. I felt as if I was going to throw up. It was hours of waiting.

The next set of x-rays was slightly different. "Here, lie down on the table and turn over on your side. Relax, while we insert this tube into your rectum and lay still," the technician told me.

"But I am going to get sick on the table," I cried.

"Please remain still, and this will be over soon." They strapped me to the motorized table, which moved me through a series of different angles. In my child's mind, I guessed that it was so the barium would move around inside me. "Lie on your side...now the other." In every different position, the table moved, too. After a few hours, we were sent home.

These tests were repeated many times throughout my childhood. The results were always the same—the cancer kept spreading.

All of my doctors decided that my family needed weekly visits with a psychiatrist, both group sessions for all of us and solo sessions for me. "There must be something terribly wrong at home to put this young child in this condition," the doctors told my parents. My parents were mortified! The doctors thought my parents had done something so terrible that I ended up as sick as I was. I overheard them one evening speaking to each other about where they went wrong in child raising and wondering what direction they should take. I heard my mother crying softly while they spoke and could not help crying myself to sleep thinking about the conversation. I loved my parents so much and thought they had given me a great childhood. There were times of disappointment when we did not get what we wanted or got punished for misbehaving, but I think all of my friends experienced the same things. How could those doctors be so mean to my parents, and what were we going to do? I found out the next morning.

As we awoke the following day and sat down to breakfast, Mom and Dad looked at my siblings and I so seriously that we were all afraid to eat. Mom spoke. "Daddy and I have decided that we are going to listen to the doctors and try to help your sister. By doing that, we must all go to the hospital on a weekly basis and talk to the doctors about our family. It might make us feel a little better inside to share with them if something is wrong, and it might even help Lisa begin to feel better. We will all take turns with the doctors, and then we will all speak to them as a family. Does everyone understand?"

She looked around the table. My younger sister, Chelle, who was only five at the time, began to giggle. Brother Jeff, who was 13, just shrugged his shoulders and kind of grunted. My guess was he had no choice. I looked at everyone, feeling responsible in some way but not sure how. It seemed like the only thing for us to do at this point, so we plugged along. Dad sat there without much to say. What could he say?

The sessions lasted about one year and only managed to make us aware of our biggest problem... living with the stress of a sick child while trying to maintain some kind of normal life. The counselor and the doctors wanted us to understand that one sick family member means that the entire family is sick. We all suffered in different ways.

Through it all, the pains I experienced managed to get worse, and my family was under more stress. As I was dragged from doctor to doctor, I did not realize that my siblings were suffering as well. My brother vied for attention by getting into trouble. He tried a little drug use, teasing us or picking fights with my sister and I, or just plain misbehaving to get my parents to pay attention to him—even if it was negative attention. No one really realized what was happening.

Almost every day, I needed attention from one parent or another— hospital trips, medications, trying to get me to eat, or holding me while I cried out in pain. The energy required was intense. I thought how difficult it must be for my parents, knowing their child might not survive. It made me incredibly sad.

Somehow, my sister managed to pull through with no hard feelings toward me—probably because she was only 4 years old when I got sick, so she did not know any better. Chelle was sent to everyone's house in the neighborhood so that my parents were freed up to care for me. Her childhood was spent playing with different kids—depending on who was watching her. She doesn't remember much of it now except that I wasn't around often.

On the other hand, my brother, who is 4 years older than I am, always treated me nicely, but he resented me at the same time. Jeff was forgotten, or so it seemed. He was already a bit troubled and constantly got into trouble vying for attention. Whatever he did caused problems, and the more problems he caused, the more my parents paid attention to him. Mom and Dad began to lose track of him. Drug experimenting, fighting with us for no reason, and getting bad grades was common behavior for him. My parents were called on a regular basis from school, and punishments did not seem to work. Jeff shared his feelings with the psychiatrists and blamed me for all of his difficulties.

Our relationship remained rocky because of this, and he commented to other family members over the years about how I was always treated better and that he was not loved as much as I was. It saddens me to this day. I am proud of his success in business but feel that his attitude toward life could be happier. He has moments of joy with his family, but his wife has shared little things with me that make me realize he still suffers and cannot seem to let go.

How very sad to hang onto something that happened when we were children. Being sick was out of my control. I could better understand if I had become self-centered and uncaring, but I *do* care very much and share whatever I can when allowed into someone's life.

CHAPTER 9

ANOREXIA

*I learned that I had become anorexic,
and this was how anorexia patients were treated.
I had to earn privileges.*

"Why won't you eat?" one doctor asked me.

"I am not hungry," was my answer.

"Do the pains go away when you don't eat?"

"No, but I have to try something," I eventually cried. I guess this is where I became stubborn. This is also where the two summers in the hospital came into play.

The first summer, at age 8, I was so ill that I was unable to function and needed to stay the entire summer months in the hospital. My mother later explained to me that the strong medications—a combination of steroids and chemotherapy—were not only fighting the bad cancer cells, they were also killing the healthy cells.

My body was unable to fight off something as simple as a cold, and I needed nourishment through intravenous feedings to help me become stronger.

The following summer, at age 9, I stopped eating completely. "No food, no bathroom" was my theory. During this particular hospital stay, I wanted to play with all the kids in the ward, but I wasn't allowed to. The rules were simple: you eat and begin to gain weight, then you can leave the bed. So I sat in my little bed with my feet unable to touch the floor. I had to bathe in bed, use a bedpan (even though I was quite capable of walking to the bathroom myself), and sit there meal after meal crying into the tray of food. I learned

25

that I had become anorexic, and this was how anorexia patients were treated. I had to earn privileges.

One hot summer day I awoke in the ward, missing my family and feeling kind of hungry. It was a strange feeling after all these months to be hungry. There were 10–15 kids in this particular ward. All of them were leaving their beds to sit at the play tables in the center of the room and eat. I was anxious to join them, and—maybe out of loneliness—I ate everything on my tray! After breakfast, I was permitted to walk to the bathroom myself. Later, I ate my lunch, and was permitted to join the other kids at playtime and eventually allowed to go out on the balcony for fresh air. I walked outside with my parents and felt the sunshine for the first time in almost 1 ½ months. I played with the outside toys and noticed that every floor in the hospital had balconies for the patients to play.

I played every day after that. There were bikes, big dollhouses, and toys to ride on all over the balcony. It felt good to have something so very simple. I wanted to be with everyone else and not alone anymore. Over time, I began to grow stronger. My parents visited me every day for hours and played with me. Sometimes we colored or painted together; other times, they just watched me with the other children.

Dad worked all day, dropping my mother off and leaving, and then came back later when he was finished. I had a trail of visitors through the summer; even some of my teachers brought me cards from my classmates or from the other teachers. My sister and brother only came a few times to visit because they were so young; children did not visit often in those days. Most of the time when my parents visited, they spoke to doctors, spoke to social workers about the bills, and assured me that I would be able to come home some day.

CHAPTER 10

THE FAMOUS DR. KOOP

Dr. Koop was very tall—massive in my eyes.
He had short hair that stood up on his head, and he wore big glasses.
His voice made me want to listen when he spoke.

You never meet the surgeon until every other option has been exhausted. After days on end as an outpatient and one psychiatrist after another, the inevitable drew near. Apparently the cancer resisted all of the drugs and began to spread, and I was deteriorating rapidly. The well-known Dr. Koop was next on our list when Dr. Rosenberg was unable to treat me anymore. We met him, and he immediately took the entire family under his wing.

I was escorted out of the examining room to play in another room while my parents spoke with Dr. Koop alone. He told them my sickness had worsened, the cancer was spreading too quickly to keep it arrested, and the disease needed to be addressed in a different manner.

"It has been two years since beginning treatment here at Children's Hospital, and Alesia is not improving," he told them. "She is getting worse. All of her doctors and I have met, studied her tests, and have come to a decision. She needs a surgery that we normally do not perform on children, but we have no choice at this time. Otherwise, she will only get worse and will probably not live past the age of 16. It is a radical surgery. I will remove her large intestine and bowel, and she will wear a 'bag' called an iliostomy for the rest of her life."

I was 10 at the time. All they could say to me was that they decided to let the doctors do what they were trained to do: save the lives of children.

Not long after that appointment, I was in Children's Hospital preparing for major surgery. I weighed 48 pounds, was extremely frail, was seriously losing my hair, and was not getting any better. I was brought into a treatment room the night before surgery, where the nurses showed me an appliance called a *bag* and all of this stuff along with it.

"Tomorrow is your operation. You will be asleep the entire time, and it will be a very long operation," one of them said. "When you awaken, you will wear this on the side of your stomach for the rest of your life."

I looked at the bag, and the next thing I knew I was on the floor. My head must have hit a filing cabinet or the floor when I fell backwards. One of the nurses helped me to my feet when I woke up a few moments later, then she escorted me back to my room. Gently crawling into bed, I felt dizzy and sick to my stomach.

"I want to see Dr. Koop right away, please," I told the nurses.

"Dr. Koop," I told him when he arrived shortly thereafter, "I want to be normal like the other kids. I cannot wear this thing on my side forever!"

Dr. Koop was very tall—massive in my eyes. He had short hair that stood up on his head, and he wore big glasses. His voice made me want to listen when he spoke. "Young lady, I will do everything I can to make you happy. We will operate, and I promise that the bag will remain as low as we can possibly place it. You have my word that I will take care of you."

We agreed on bikini-low for the spot to place the appliance, and he assured me that no one but me would ever know it was there. I was so sick, but the most unimportant thing—vanity—was important to me.

The doctor had a wonderful bedside manner and was sensitive to all of my needs. It was more important to save my life than to take care of any cosmetic, superficial concerns, yet Dr. Koop respected my wishes and did a wonderful job concealing my scars.

My parents waited hours for surgery to be over. It must have been hard for them. Being the patient is easier because you're asleep the entire time. Sitting, watching the clock for 8–10 hours, and waiting for the operating room doors to open and hear a nurse or doctor call their child's name was absolutely brutal for my parents.

After recovery, I went to a special ward strictly for heart patients. In the days of my first surgeries, the Children's Hospital had no air conditioning, but heart patients needed to be kept cool. There were six beds, all full, with just one window unit for all of us.

I woke up in a fog and tried to speak. "Mom…Dad…am I okay?" I said with a hoarse voice barely clear enough to understand.

"Yes," they answered together, reaching to hold my hand. They looked at me with tears in their eyes. "You are going to be fine, just go back to sleep. We are both here if you need anything," they told me. I dozed on and off for days. Every time I woke, they were there watching over me.

"I feel pain a little," I cried to them many times. "Can you get the nurse to give me more medicine?" Every three hours, I received shots for pain either in my thighs or my butt. They had to be given in fatty spots, but they were difficult to find on me because of my frail frame.

At the time of my first surgery, the pain medicine knocked me out for a few hours. If I had pain before the three hours were up, I watched the clock until time for the next injection. Sometimes the pain grew intense, but I had to wait. I adjusted to my wait for medication like all the other children in the room—I was not alone in my misery.

CHAPTER 11

COULD I GET ANY SICKER?

Everyone brought me gifts, but I was so sick that I really didn't care.

After several days post-surgery and a sea of visitors, I again became extremely ill. With a 105-degree fever, something was obviously wrong. Tests discovered a collapsed lung. The nurses gently rolled me from side to side to place me on an ice bed. I spent two entire days watching a regular looking bucket full of ice hanging next to my bed. As it melted, it drained to the special mat placed beneath me to reduce my high fever. I shivered and cried but was not allowed to be moved from the ice bed. Dr. Koop checked on me constantly, and although I cried to him, he was unable to help me. He comforted me, as my parents did, but other visitors were not permitted until I was stable. I spent most of the day watching the nurses go back and forth, dozing off, and talking to my mother and father. After two days, the fever dropped.

The next thing I remember was being taken by wheelchair to the examining room where I had fainted. *What else could they do to me? What was left?* Dr. Koop was there as I was helped onto the table in the center of the room.

"Young lady, you have a collapsed lung," he said. "This is probably the result of the extreme fever, so we are going to draw the fluid out of your lung and see if it will help you breathe a bit easier. Sit and let your feet hang over the side of the table," he told me.

I was frightened but did as I was told. I trusted him.

"Now, we are going to draw fluid from your lung, so you will need to sit very still and not move—no matter what. Do you understand?" he asked as he pulled out a very large needle. His voice was very stern, and I took him quite seriously. As he inserted the needle into my back, I cried and screamed. I even called him a jerk, but I did not move. Quickly the procedure was over, and I was wheeled back to my little room.

The first time I looked down at my belly and saw the bag hanging from it, I felt kind of ill. *Can this be how I am going to look forever? What am I going to tell my friends, and how can I hide this thing!?*

My nurses taught me how to change the bag and empty it when it was full. "How can I do this myself?" I asked.

"It will become a habit each morning—like brushing your teeth," one of my nurses explained on the first morning we tried to empty the thing. There was an opening at the bottom of the bag that stayed sealed until the bag was emptied in the bathroom. Special glue held the other end to my belly to protect anything from leaking out of the sides. Waste was then tunneled into the bag.

The bag was odorless and small enough to hide, and it held quite a bit of waste. When it needed to be emptied, we headed to the bathroom together to give it a try. I emptied it into the toilet, sealed the bottom again, and washed my hands.

"My head feels a little dizzy," I told my nurse. "Am I okay?"

She seemed to understand that I was a little upset about my first experience. "Just sit down on your bed for a few minutes," she told me. "You will get used to your new way of life."

I did as she told me but still could not accept that this was forever. "Please ask Dr. Koop if someday they can replace all of my organs removed with an animal's," I continued. "Do you think that could ever happen?" I asked her.

"Right now, something like that is not even a thought," said my nurse. "I will let Dr. Koop know what you have asked, but you need to concentrate on taking care of yourself and getting healthy."

We practiced changing the new bag and emptying it almost every day together after that, and I was eventually on my own and did not need much help from my nurses.

During follow-up x-rays, I was told I needed another surgery to remove more cancer that they missed the first time. Recovery became another very long hospital stay because problems began to pop up.

For about two months, my hospital room consisted of a bed, nightstand, and curtain. I laid there—very content with or without visitors—surrounded by enough "get well" cards that they became like wallpaper, stuck to every bare section of wall and covering the chipping paint. Everyone brought me gifts, but I was so sick that I really didn't care.

My family adjusted to my environment but looked forward to heading home. Mom and dad came to visit often but had two other children at home to attend to. I think they spent very little time with Chelle and Jeff and most of their time with me or waiting to speak to the doctors. After about two months, I was finally dismissed and returned home.

CHAPTER 12

A NEW HOME LIFE

*...we were put in touch with a support group who was able to guide
us all into this new life and provide insight into self-care.*

When I finally arrived home, my parents were in charge of my care. My first few days with the bag attached to my side were truly a challenge. Of course, we really had no clue how to handle the situation, so we spent large amounts of time traveling back and forth to the hospital. Finally, we were put in touch with a support group who was able to guide us all into this new life and provide insight into self-care. I adjusted better than my parents—being young seems to make it easier to adjust to anything—but my siblings were clueless as to my needs. Who could blame them? They were children.

The following summer, fully recovered, our family rented a small apartment in Atlantic City. We could finally spend the summer together as a family near the beach and boardwalk. One day, I was in the apartment eating a plum, and the small pit slipped down my throat. I knew immediately that I would not be able to pass it through the only intestine I had, and I began to panic. Within hours, I began having sharp pains and could barely walk. My parents took me to the Atlantic City Medical Center where they removed my bag while I screamed and cried out in pain.

"I can see the tip of the plum pit," I told the doctor. "Can you just grab it and pull it out?" The doctor said that was not possible. He instead inserted a tube into the stoma on the side of my stomach. A "stoma" is a small piece of intestine that is surgically placed outside your body to attach the bag. The pain was so very bad that after 12 hours of them telling my mother they needed to do surgery, we left for Philadelphia. We decided to go back to The Children's Hospital in Philadelphia where they were familiar with my case. It was about an hour and a half from Atlantic City to Philadelphia,

When we entered the emergency room there, I was so weak that my father had to carry me in and place me on the gurney. Nurses brought me into a room and within minutes the pit was removed with an instrument that looked like delicate tweezers. I was admitted for a night for dehydration and trauma, but I was back on my feet again after a few days with a new lesson learned: Be aware of what I eat, chew very carefully, and take my time!

CHAPTER 13

MORE SURGERY

I scanned the medical magazines and BINGO—
I found what I thought I was looking for.

"This is brilliant," I told my parents as I began to show them what I had discovered. Both parents, although a bit leery, learned to be open minded to my ideas. "I may not be able to have my intestinal track replaced, but they could build a bag out of my own tissues. It would rest on my uterus," I told them, "and my body would not be able to reject it because it would be made out of my own tissue. Oh my God, this could be the normal life I have been looking for!"

The first time I discovered the option, I was around 11 or 12 years old. My drive was there because without Internet or cell phones to connect us to the entire world, I depended on whatever reading material my parents had coming to our home. I scanned the medical magazines and BINGO—I found what I thought I was looking for.

Once convinced, my parents took me to see Dr. Koop at Children's Hospital. I remember entering his office for the first time after so many years. I stepped into his large, masculine office and saw Dr. Koop sitting behind an oversized desk. Before I even explained why I was there, I looked behind him at the large, beautiful photo of a young man on top of a mountain, posing with one leg bent like he was conquering it. We were told later by his secretary that the young man in the photo was Dr. Koop's son, who was killed in a climbing accident not long after the photo was taken. Dr. Koop went into seclusion for quite some time after it happened. She also told us that he had taken it especially hard because he had skillful enough hands to heal the sickest of children, but he did not have any control over his own son's loss of life.

I remember feeling very sad when I heard this, and I nearly cried thinking how painful this must have been to the doctor who had become my hero.

In his office, I tried to explain to Dr. Koop what I had learned, and his explanation was straight and direct. "Alesia, my dear, this surgery is not being done in the United States at this time. And after all you have been through, you are crazy to even think about it." Done and over—he had nothing more to say.

I was determined. When I turned 14 or 15, I went back with the exact same ideas and questions. "Dr. Koop, please understand that I want to be normal like the other kids my age, and now the surgery I spoke to you about a few years ago is being done in the United States."

Dr. Koop listened but said, "Alesia, my dear, you need to wait until your body has matured. Sixteen years of age will be a better time. Also, your weight will have to increase by 30 pounds for us to have extra skin and fat to work with."

I was very thin at the time but not sickly. Dr. Koop was such a serious person when he spoke. To cheer him up, I put smiley face stickers on my "bag" so he would always see a smile while examining me. He did his exam, saw my smiley faces on the bag, and grinned a very wide grin.

"Okay, you win. We will do this surgery...but first you have to be a bit older and grow a little."

Dr. Koop had me come to the office one day for an exam while we waited for me to be old enough for the next surgery. I recall three medical students sitting in that big office staring at me. I was told not to say anything about who I was or what was wrong with me, and their job was to guess my ailment. It was a wonderful feeling since I was very clever in the way I dressed. Dr. Koop beamed as if I were his child. In some strange way, I think all of his patients were his children, and saving our lives was a rebirth for him.

All three medical students focused on me. After about 20 guesses, he had me show them my surgical area (and, of course, my smiley faces). Dr. Koop had a sense of humor and seemed proud to show me off to his students.

Although it was wonderful to be able to hide what was wrong with me,

I still had a drive to learn more about the new Kock Pouch surgery and wanted to have it done. I was healthy and thriving as a teen, but I felt I would be closer to "normal" not having this thing hanging off my belly for the rest of my life. I did not have many choices, so I kept reading and learning about the new surgery.

CHAPTER 14

LEARNING MORE ABOUT MY HERO

I thought at that moment how very special this man was.

I questioned Dr. Koop once about his son's death. He told me, "I only understand saving lives, and I take it very seriously. Death is very difficult to comprehend for me because I believe everyone has a right to live no matter what is wrong with them."

As we sat in his office talking, he recalled a child born with all of her internal organs on the outside. While the doctors thought it was hopeless for this baby, Dr. Koop felt very strongly about giving her a chance at life. After many hours in surgery, all of her organs were repositioned as best as possible. With some humor and thought he said, "I even made her a little bellybutton." He chuckled as he described it to me, saying, "It is a little off to the side but at least she will look down and have one."

I thought at that moment how very special this man was.

During one of my many stays at the hospital, he managed to get me into the intensive care unit to see Siamese twins that he had just separated. It was a first for him at the time, and I think for Children's Hospital. I got to peek at them in an area where no one was permitted. Dr. Koop snuck me up a side stair to look at them for a minute. They were so small and frail, but they were alive.

Two years later, after they returned to their country and were celebrating their birthday, one twin choked on a balloon and died. Dr. Koop again secluded himself for a period of time. It was a senseless death, considering that the child had survived so very much.

I remember feeling a great sadness in hearing the news of the death. It gave me a sense of how very delicate our lives are from one moment to the next. "How can anyone, especially a parent who has been through what they had been through, carry on?" I asked Dr. Koop. He looked at me with a brief but clear blank stare and said, "Alesia, my dear, life is more precious than you may ever realize. We all need to step back and use these moments to reflect on everything we have and to appreciate life."

CHAPTER 15

WHERE DO I FIT IN?

*My illness was a blessing that taught me at an early age
to appreciate all that I had in life, so I was able to let things go
quicker than most people were.*

I struggled to return to a kid's life, and I always felt different from that time on. I looked at the world from a different perspective than other kids, which I assume is from all the pain and suffering I went through. I did not get upset about everyday things that other kids got rattled about. When my friends gossiped about 'this girl did this' and 'this boy did that,' I thought they were being ridiculous. I was more concerned about how sad it was when I went to the hospital for a visit and saw so many sick children and their families.

These were times when Dr. Koop's words weighed on me—about how precious life was and not to take anything for granted. My illness was a blessing that taught me at an early age to appreciate all that I had in life, so I was able to let things go quicker than most people were.

As I grew older, I imagined teaching delinquent children a lesson by taking them to The Children's Hospital of Philadelphia for a day to see and experience firsthand what suffering and sickness was really like. Getting a glimpse of what chronically ill children deal with would change anyone's perspective.

I remained a patient of Children's Hospital for seven years and underwent surgical procedures for other minor complications due to my condition. I was fortunate to remain cancer free and developed into a young teenager.

At around 14 years old, I began to menstruate, a little behind my friends, but that was due to the cancer slowing my maturity.

What a difference this time when I called out to my mother from the bathroom again. This was more exciting—I got to ask for my mother's help. "Mom, can you come here a minute?" I yelled out to her. I was in the upstairs bathroom again. My heart was beating fast, my hands were a little shaky, and I felt a bit scared, but with a rush of adrenaline.

"Yes," she called out to me. "What is it Lisa? Are you okay?" I could hear her footsteps rushing toward the bathroom, probably worried that she'd find something horrible happening behind the door.

"I'm fine," I called out. "Quick, come in! I have to ask you something. I got my period. Oh my god, I finally got my period! Everyone else has it, and I thought I would never get it."

Mom stepped back to give me some space. She reached under the sink to her supply of feminine products and began to shuffle through them. When I looked at her and our eyes met, she had a big smile on her face as if I had done the most wonderful thing.

"I have to tell you," she began, "when you called me to come to the bathroom, my heart skipped a beat. You have no idea for that split second how I felt—and how happy I am now that you are okay. I am as thrilled as you are," she continued. "Now you are truly a woman. I will show you what you need to do to take care of yourself." The smile on her face made me relax instantly.

"Let's go tell Grandmom!" I yelled.

My grandmother was visiting us that week when we rushed downstairs to tell her the strangest thing happened. "Guess what, Grandmom!" I cried out to her in the living room. "I got my period!" I was beaming at this point.

Grandmom walked up to me and slapped my face. It did not hurt, but it caught me off guard. "What was that for?" I asked.

"It's good luck," my mother replied while headed down the stairs. "It's something a grandmother does to welcome you into womanhood."

CHAPTER 16

MY BEST FRIENDS

Ours was a rare friendship that many people dream about but few experience.

"Let's take a road trip to Florida to see Sandra in Miami," Randee said one day while we were watching television at her house. "On the way, we can explore different places by car." Randee had bright red curly hair and glasses. If anyone looked dorky as a kid, it was her. She was always a bit chunky, so together we traveled through teenage-hood yo-yo dieting like most girls. We grew into lifelong buddies, shared all of our thoughts and dreams, spent every weekend together, played, watched television, went to dances, and developed a relationship that was a rare jewel. Randee and I still keep in touch, and although we rarely see one another, our friendship is one that makes time stand still.

Sandra's dark hair and skin looked oriental to us. She was extremely thin but ate like a horse. All of us were born on the same street, but I was two years younger than Sandra and Randee. We had been friends from as far back as I could remember and spent all of our free time together, playing, eating, shopping, coloring, and sleeping over at each others' houses. Daydreaming was something we did well as a threesome

"We'll probably live together with our husbands when we are older, right?" I used to say often. Randee and Sandra would chime in that we might even marry brothers. When we got older, we went roller-skating at the local rink every Friday or went to neighborhood dances where we could look for boys. Then Sandra went off to college.

By the time Randee and I were ready for our road trip, Nick and I had broken up. I was 16 and a bit melancholy about the breakup, but Randee persuaded me to go. I looked forward to getting away and not thinking about Nick any more.

"Now all we have to do is convince our parents that we can handle this trip to Florida and that we will be okay," was my answer as we chatted. I knew I was usually able to talk my parents into letting me do stuff, but this was bigger than anything I had ever asked for.

"I'll babysit any time I need to Mom, for anyone in the neighborhood, and use all my own money for this trip, I swear!" I pleaded. "I'll clean my room, do the dishes, help around the house—anything!"

Randee was in the same boat, bugging her mother. She kept me posted on what they spoke about. "My mother thinks we are too young to drive all that way to Florida," she would constantly tell me. "She thinks we may get lost and something will happen to us. What does she think will happen? It's a straight road almost all the way to Miami."

My answer to Randee was always the same. "We can do this, I know we can. What could possibly happen? We have a big car, a CB radio to call for help if we break down, and locks on the hotel room doors."

After two or three months of constantly bugging them, they all agreed to let us take the trip. We were so excited we wanted to scream, but instead we concentrated on planning and figuring out how to make it work financially. Halfway through the summer, we were packing the car for Daytona Beach, Disney World, and Miami. Our plan was to drive our car on the beach in Daytona, experience Disney World, and head for our final destination: Miami. Randee's uncle owned a hotel there, and we could stay free while we visited Sandra, who was attending college in the area.

Our parents packed us food for the road, which we finished before we even got out of New Jersey, but we had money and clothing, and we were ready. We had both been on family trips before, but this was the first time we were each going to be away from our families for this long—almost the entire month of August.

The first day we drove for at least ten hours. We finally stopped along the road and checked into a motel. We felt a bit scared doing this on our own as we stood in the lobby with money in hand.

"We need a room for one night," Randee told the clerk, and a few minutes later we had our room keys. It should have been simple, but figuring out what we needed to bring in from the car for one night seemed to be a problem. We opened the trunk. "Okay, we need our clothes, enough for a change, the cooler with the leftover food, the CB radio and handbags," we both said, talking over each other. By the time we got to the room, we had just about everything out of the trunk, including the 50-pound suitcase with no wheels on it. We laughed so much we could barely walk.

We got into the room, got comfy, found a restaurant, and had dinner. Back in the room later that night, Randee headed toward the bathroom. "Oh my god!" she screamed and ran to me in the bedroom.

"What?!"

"There is a giant bug in the tub!"

"Kill it!"

"You kill it!"

"Not me!"

Holding each other and trembling, we headed into the bathroom with a few magazines, which we threw at the thing, but it would not die.

"Let's call the front desk for help," I told her.

"Great idea," she said quickly.

We surely could not conquer this task on our own. When the guy arrived, he looked at us like we were crazy, walked into the bathroom, killed the bug and exited. When he left, we were both in the bedroom practically hugging each other out of fear.

We left bright and early the next morning. Our first big stop was South of the Border. In the planning stages, we had chosen this destination as our first big stop. On the border between North and South Carolina, it was so much more than your average rest stop. It seemed like such a neat place to visit and kind of like a halfway mark to Florida. While driving on Route 95, it kind of became a game to follow the "South of the Border" billboards that advertised this place as a sort of paradise.

Since it was our first big car trip, we arrived with as much enthusiasm as we could—happy to be halfway into our trip. It turned out to be a few acres of shops, restaurants, and hotels. South of the Border was truly not a destination, but more of a fuel stop for both gas and food. The excitement was quickly lost when we realized it was just a glamorized tourist stop. We did not really mind though; we had arrived!

We got there at 9:00 a.m. and realized that we could eat whatever we wanted and that no one was there to tell us differently. Randee decided on chili for breakfast, and I agreed it was a good idea. We made it a short stop to stretch our legs, and off we went to the next destination.

When we arrived in Daytona Beach, it seemed important to us to drive that car on the beach. Imagine, we drove hundreds of miles just to drive in the sand. This was something we had heard about and decided to put it on our list of adventures while driving through Florida.

We pulled the car onto the beach. Others were either riding around or parked, so we had to be careful. Randee took a deep breath and slowly began to drive on the sand. We thought we were so cool because we were doing exactly as we had set out to do. After staying over in Daytona for a single night, we headed out.

Disney World was only one park at that time, but that was enough to keep a couple of teens occupied for two or three days. We checked into the hotel, emptied the car again, and went off to the pool. I think part of the plan was constantly working up a good appetite! For someone who had spent several years intentionally not eating in my teens, food became one of the greatest joys in my life. Randee shared my enthusiasm, and we never missed a chance to eat!

"Let's eat french fries, burgers, ice cream, water ice, lemonade and candy," we squealed to each other. We rode every ride as if we had never been to a park before, saw every show we could, and took every possible adventure. We did it all! We left Disney with big smiles and a great feeling of satisfaction before heading to Miami.

"Let's call home and check in with our parents," Randee suggested before we left.

"Good idea. I'll call my mom and dad first," I told her. We had checked in from each stop we made, but we were having so much fun at Disney World that we forgot to call.

"Mom, we're okay and having a ball," I said. "The weather is perfect, and someday I might want to live down here."

"Well, let's get you through school first," she replied. "I am glad you are having a great time. Are you being careful? Please be very cautious!"

Randee checked in with her mom as well. "Yes, we are being careful, and we're headed for Miami to Uncle Bob's place. We will check in after we get settled in, okay? Talk to you then, and I love you..."

The hotel belonging to Randee's Uncle turned out to be a dump where everyone was—or looked to be—100 years old. We went food shopping since we had a little kitchen and even littler funds. It was a lot for a couple of suburban teens, and we managed to get along pretty well. We had never spent this much time together; the extended period sometimes tested our friendship.

Randee was a redhead with alabaster white skin, and I worshipped the sun. I would use pure baby oil every time we were out and absorb as much sun as my skin could take. Randee, on the other hand, would screen every exposed body part and sometimes sit under an umbrella. I felt bad for her— having to always protect herself from the sun—but if she did not, the burn would be so bad that it would make her very ill. The only other difference I recall is that Randee was always running late. It was very rare that she would be ready on time or before me. I was extremely prompt, and we clashed at times because of this, but we managed to overcome these issues and try to work around them.

The most important thing about my friendship with Randee was that she was there for me through it all. She dropped everything to be by my side and help me through each obstacle in my life. It was never too much for Randee. Ours was a rare friendship that many people dream about but few experience.

Sandra was the same age as Randee, both about two years older than me. She had gone to Miami for fashion school and looked the part when we went for our first visit. She was slim, well dressed and a bit more mature than at home. But she was still our good friend, and we were there to spend time hanging out with her.

It was strange to be visiting Sandra in a different setting than we were used to as children. We looked forward to this visit all summer while we saved our money for this trip. When we finally got the chance to see her, we were a bit nervous. She was still our leader—similar to when we were growing up. Both Randee and I always looked up to her and admired her savvy, like being bold enough to move this far away from home to attend school.

Sandra had a few roommates but very little money, and she looked forward to going to dinner with any guy who would pay so she could fill up, eating as much as she could handle. "You see," she explained, "if I eat all the bread, and all the food they put in front of me, then I don't have to worry about buying food for a while."

"Don't you think that's kind of strange?" Randee asked her.

"I agree," I said. "Why not get some money from your mom for food so you don't have to worry about eating? Seems strange not to know when you are going to eat again, don't you think?"

"My mother gives me a monthly allowance, but I try to save it for other things like clothes," Sandra told us. "When it runs out, I don't want her to know because I'm afraid she'll make me come home. I want her to think everything is okay, and I can do this without too much help. Understand?"

This seemed so bizarre to me. When we were growing up, we all enjoyed the comfort of home cooked family dinners nightly and hanging out at each other's houses. We never had to think about when we were going to eat, yet now she was living meal-to-meal. Randee and I could not understand, but we were able to relate to Sandra's feeling of wanting to stay away at school. Randee and I both thought how odd it was that Sandra was behaving like this. She hadn't been gone long enough to have changed so much.

That night, Sandra took us to the nightclubs even though we were all underage. Legal drinking age at the time was 19 years old, so it was easier to sneak into clubs when we were dressed up. Sandra spent all night dancing—she was a wonderful dancer, with her slim body and beautiful dark hair. She seemed to have outgrown us a bit, probably maturing from being away at school. Looking back, I think I felt jealous. Sandra had all the freedom in the world, and her mother did not know anything except what Sandra told her.

"I feel uncomfortable with her living arrangements and the fact that she has no money or food in the refrigerator," Randee confided. "Something isn't right."

I knew what she meant. If Sandra's mother knew she had no money or food she would have had a heart attack; her mother was quite strict about everything she did, ate, and wore. Her mom watched over her very carefully, just like our parents did. Still, Sandra was not the same girl we once knew.

"She's acting like she has it all figured out, but to me it looks distorted," I told Randee. I felt funny watching her new lifestyle and knowing we had to keep quiet about what we saw, especially to our parents. We visited with her a few more times during our weeks in Florida and left with an uneasy feeling that neither of us really understood.

"This is probably one of the first big secrets we have to keep from our parents," I brought up to Randee one day before we left Florida.

"You're right," she answered, quite upset. "Sandra's behavior is off, and we can't even rat on her," she replied.

CHAPTER 17

A PAINFUL EXPERIENCE

First love is first love. I was wiser for the next relationship.

I had been working at the Brigantine Castle prior to meeting Nicky (and lied about my age). It was just before my 15th birthday, and at that point, to avoid getting into trouble, I couldn't tell anyone my true age. As a result, I kept up the lie, was hired by Nicky to work the carnival games, and began dating him at the same time.

My mother liked him and trusted me with him, so I was allowed to do much more than other kids my age. We went to dinner, and I had no problem getting served alcohol. Nick thought I was 16, so I began to believe it myself. It was an easy white lie until my Sweet 16th birthday, when I wanted to show him off to my friends.

"Nick, there's something you need to know about me," I told him one night when we were alone.

"Nothing that you say ever bothers me," he said.

"I am only 15 and going to be 16 very soon. I want you to know so you can celebrate my birthday with me."

Nick was quiet for a moment. He looked at me in such a strange way that I thought he was going to yell at me.

"Stand back and let me look at you," he said. "You are only 15 years old?"

"Yes, and I am sorry I misled you. When I came for a job, I needed to be 16 so I had to lie," I explained. "I never knew that we would become this close. I am sorry," I repeated.

From that moment on, we were even closer. Nick was able to be part of

49

my special birthday, and over the next two years, I became closer with his sisters and his mother. For a long time, he even drove two hours to pick me up for weekends at his mother's house. After the first year of dating, I was able to give up my virginity to him without guilt and felt fortunate my first love understood about the differences in my body.

Our relationship blossomed, and Nick took me out often to bars and nightclubs. I was never asked for an ID and he seemed to know everyone anyway. My favorite night out was in New York when we went to see Barry White at Radio City Music Hall. Nick and I were part of a handful of white people among thousands at the concert, and we had a blast.

One day, I knocked on his apartment door. His roommate Drew answered but said, "Nick is sleeping, come back later."

I was puzzled. "I just dropped by.... I'll wake him up."

Drew blocked me from coming in, but I managed to maneuver around him. When I got to the bedroom door, he stood in front of me and said, "You don't want to go in there right now, Alesia. Please understand."

I was numb for a few moments and stared at the door, not sure what to do next.

"Are you okay?" Drew asked.

"Of course, I am fine, I think," but tears swelled into my eyes, and he could see I was far from okay. I ran down the stairs and jumped into my car. Not knowing where I was headed, I drove to the beach a few blocks away and jumped out of the car, shaking and crying. I walked down to the water, trying to clear my head and think about what just happened.

Giving up my virginity was such a big thing! I trusted everything about him and wanted to continue to trust him as our love grew.

Nick's sisters later confessed that they knew he had been cheating on me for awhile, but they were afraid to tell me the details. They feared what would happen if he had found out who told.

Nick and I managed to get back together for a short time over the next year, but things were never quite the same. First love is first love. I was wiser for the next relationship.

Looking back, Nick and I thought we had a lot in common. We certainly had fun together, but Nick made most of the decisions, and I was willing to play on his terms. As I grew older and had other relationships, I learned that I had a voice—and I would use it (quite loudly!).

CHAPTER 18

A MAJOR SETBACK

◦◦◦

The tables had now turned again, and I suddenly
understood what my parents had experienced for so long—
watching someone you love suffer.

While I was trying to gain weight and read up on my impending surgery, I went to Children's Hospital for a conference about the new Kock Pouch. One of the kids I met through my volunteer work at the hospital asked to come along. Her name was Miriam, and she was my age. When we met, she was also interested in the same new surgery. My mother, and a therapist named Stella that my family had become close to, took Miriam and I to learn more about this new procedure. We never made it to the meeting, though. As our friend Stella reached out to get the ticket at the top of the parking lot, she pressed the accelerator instead of the brake. The car veered over the edge and tumbled down to the lower level, hitting the walls on either side all the way down. My mother was the front passenger, and Miriam and I were in the back seat.

I heard screams all the way down, then we violently crashed into a concrete wall. It happened quickly—I saw smoke and (I think) fire. People were running toward us. Miriam was smashed up against me on one side of the car, and my head felt like a sledge hammer had hit me. I heard my mother screaming that she could not move. "Help me!" she cried. "Someone help me! I can't move! It's hot in here!"

Stella was pinned to the wheel and screaming as well. I managed to open my door and fell out of the car. Even though I felt compelled to get away from the smoke and fire quickly, I knew my mother needed me. Miriam landed on top of me and we rolled over. Someone helped us to the side of the lot.

"My mother needs me, where is she?" I cried.

I felt someone take my hand and walk Miriam and me away from the vehicle and through a tunnel under the hospital. It was a blur: I was crying. We all were. Two gurneys went by and I guessed it was my mother and Stella. Minutes turned to hours, and my father was suddenly there.

"Who called you?" I asked him when he approached me. "How did they find you?" His face was very serious.

"Mom is bad, and she will need lots of surgery," he continued. "I am so glad you're okay. We need to concentrate on Mom, do you understand?"

After taking x-rays, the doctors determined that Miriam and I were fine. Did the back seat save our lives? I wondered as I sat with my dad.

Eventually, we were allowed to go home. Stella was admitted with a broken leg and my mother was in surgery. The doctors promised to keep my dad posted through the night, but he needed to take me home so I could rest.

Mom spent three to four months in the hospital with broken ribs, a broken wrist, and a broken leg. The motor came into the car on impact and burned a hole in the back of her foot as well. Again, life took a drastic turn for my entire family. I visited her as often as possible, and watching her suffer made me so sad. I helped care for her after she came home, along with working part time and going to high school. The tables had now turned again, and I suddenly understood what my parents had experienced for so long— watching someone you love suffer.

"Dad, is mom going to ever be okay?" I asked him one day while we cleaned up the dinner dishes.

"I don't know if or when she will be the mom we remember," he said. At least he was honest with me. The next few months, my father and I became much closer. He depended on me to help with my little sister and care for my mother. Mom regained her strength after about six months, but she never really was the same despite resuming her role as mother and housewife.

CHAPTER 19

PREPARING FOR
ANOTHER SURGERY

There was no way I was living my entire life with that bag on.
I just never accepted it; refused to.

My body was more adult when I was 17 years old.

"Although you are healthy at this point of your life," Dr. Koop explained, "the new surgery will require using your own tissues to build a pouch that will rest on your uterus. This extra tissue and fat from your weight gain will provide us skin and fat to work with. By using your own tissue, your body won't reject the surgery."

It was a lot for me to comprehend.

He continued. "You will need a younger set of hands for this surgery, more steady and skilled in case problems arise. I am preparing to leave medicine, but Dr. Templeton will be an excellent surgeon for you. I will arrange for you to meet him and plan this operation."

Transitioning from a frail little girl to a 130-pound teen was an odd experience. I spent most of my time concentrating on what fattening foods I could eat: pizza, ice cream, hoagies, sweets, and big portions of everything. It was a struggle in the beginning to allow myself to eat large portions and finish everything. Over a period of 6-8 months, I managed to gain the weight needed for this special surgery, but being heavy felt foreign to me. I needed to move into bigger clothes but tried not to purchase too much because I was not planning to remain that round!

I recall the mindset I had at such a young age. There was no way I was living my entire life with that bag on. I just never accepted it; refused to. At the age of ten, nearly dying from colitis and having no other options, I should have been content to be safe and healthy. But I would not settle for anything less than being "normal," and I was determined to make it work.

About one month later, I met Dr. Templeton to begin planning my surgery. I did not realize it at the time, but Dr. Templeton was analyzing me for the procedure during our meeting. He needed to be certain that I understood the responsibility that accompanied such a surgery. If the doctors built a pouch inside of me, I would have to use a catheter to eliminate waist and would not have the option of whether or not to use it. At all times, I would have to carry medical supplies with me.

CHAPTER 20

EⳲPERIENCING DEATH

"I must be in a terrible dream, right Mom?"

On the night before I checked into the hospital for surgery, some of my friends gathered at my home. The phone rang over our laughter.

My mother answered it—then began to cry and turned to face us with the phone still in her hand.

"Mom, what's wrong? What is it? What happened?" I asked her nervously. "Mom, please…"

Randee turned toward her, and we both rose from our seats on the couch. My mother said, "Sit down."

My mom was my girlfriends' favorite mother. She was the coolest of all the other moms, and my friends told her everything. She was like a best friend to them, giving advice but still earning their respect. She had a wonderful lighthearted personality, laughed and cried easily, and cared for my friends as if they were her own children.

"Your friend Sandra was in a terrible accident. She and some friends piled into a van leaving one nightclub headed to another," she told us slowly as if she needed to gather her thoughts as she spoke. "Her mother is not certain if she even knew the driver of the van, but he was traveling on I-95 in Ft. Lauderdale at a very high rate of speed. The wind caught the van and flipped it over. Everyone in the overcrowded van was thrown out… all over the highway," she told us with tears in her eyes.

At that moment, my life again changed. I felt as if I was dreaming and could not control my crying. Randee was worse than I was, and our other friends left because we were so upset.

"We need to go right to Florida," I told Randee and my mother through my sobbing. "I have to cancel my surgery and be there for her." I looked around my house. "I must be in a terrible dream, right Mom?" Our home began to close in on me, and my mother reacted right away.

My mother walked toward me, noticing the look on my face. "I feel like I am going to be sick," I told her.

"Randee, you need to go home, and we can all talk about this tomorrow. Sandra's mother Helen is flying down with her other daughter Donna tonight and will get back to us as soon as they know more details. As for your surgery, Lisa, you have planned this for so very long, you cannot back out now. We will keep you updated on Sandra's health. She is unconscious and on life support, but if she were here, she would agree with me. Do you understand?"

"I don't know what to do."

"Just calm down and try to get some sleep," she told me.

I did not close my eyes that entire night. I kept thinking about packing a bag and just taking off without anyone knowing. The next morning, I headed to the hospital for a procedure that would better my life while one of my closest friends laid in a Florida hospital dying.

CHAPTER 21

A NEW BEGINNING

⌒〜⌒

Being wheeled into surgery, I was excited and extremely nervous.

The next morning, we went to Children's Hospital for surgery. My surgeon and the other doctors knew what had happened to us the night before. I tried to clear my head to prepare for the undertaking I was about to go through.

As my parents and I followed the nurse to the floor where I would spend the next ten days or so, I glanced to my left and spied the little hospital chapel. For a split second, I felt a chill as I peeked into the room and saw the candles burning. It brought back a special memory of Sandra, Randee and me on Christmas morning. Sandra gave me a candle several years ago on Christmas— it was so simple, so small, yet so pretty and thoughtful. I loved Sandra and all she stood for. How would I ever survive if I could not see her face again?

My mind wandered to pleasant memories. Christmas as young teens, with five dollars, each of us managed to find a special something for each other.

"You are all invited over tonight to help decorate the Christmas tree," Sandra told us one week before Christmas.

"We would love to help!" Randee and I gushed. We did not realize the amount of work that went into purchasing the perfect tree and decorating it.

"Can we do anything we want? " I asked Sandra.

"No, I will give you direction as to where all of the ornaments should go. Each ornament has a story, and a special meaning to our family. My mom will help, too," she told us.

Sandra seemed to be our leader and I am not sure who made the rules, but they worked for us. After decorating, we went to a gift shop that carried all kinds of affordable knickknacks, where we spent hours looking for that "special something."

Entering the hospital and passing the tiny chapel, I could not stop thinking of that one day with Sandra. Tears rolled down my face as I followed my parents and the nurses down the hall. My thoughts raced ahead to my surgery. I was about to be given a new chance at a healthy life, I thought—yet Sandra's future was uncertain. I tried to push the negative thoughts away and instead, surround myself with memories of the holidays, the smiles, and being with family and friends.

We grew up in a predominantly Jewish neighborhood. Since Sandra was catholic, we embraced her and her family and their holiday. We looked forward to the special cookies her mother baked and placed on the dining room table in such large quantities that we gathered there just about every day during the holidays to get our fill. The closeness and the twinkle of the lights felt warm and cozy. I suddenly missed those days. It saddened me that growing up with Sandra had ended and that she was in a hospital bed far away, but I took warm memories of her with me to surgery.

I joked with my surgeon, Dr. Templeton, before surgery the next morning. "Hey, since I am the first one in this hospital to have this surgery, are you going to use an instruction manual?"

Despite his usual good sense of humor, he was too serious to joke back. "I think I am going to be fine. I know what I am doing."

Dr. Templeton and Dr. Koop were leaders in surgery at The Children's Hospital of Philadelphia, and they both accomplished amazing advances in surgical procedures. I later realized that Dr. Koop was preparing to retire soon after my surgery to become the Surgeon General of the United States. I was blessed with his friendship, and my body was blessed by his brilliance.

Being wheeled into surgery, I was excited and extremely nervous. I was taken into the operating room after kissing my mother and father goodbye. "See you in a few hours," I smiled and squeezed their hands while the orderlies patiently waited.

"Good luck and sweet dreams," said my mother. I could see the anxiety on her face as she watched the bed roll away. Dad held onto her, as she was still unsteady on her feet following the accident.

In the operating room, I was moved to the operating table. It was freezing, and I began to tremble.

"Do you want a warm blanket?" the nurse asked when she saw my teeth chattering.

"Please. Thank you. That would be great," I told her. The blanket was so warm and toasty draped over my body that I instantly started to relax and surveyed my surroundings. My arms were strapped down, and everyone was preparing the trays and tables. Standing at the head of the table was the anesthesiologist getting ready and I looked into his eyes and smiled a bit. He paused his conversation for a moment and looked directly at me.

"Okay, Alesia, what flavor do you want to go to sleep with?" he asked. "We have watermelon, strawberry, root beer, banana, and chocolate."

"Um, how about root beer!" I requested.

"No problem. Now relax, count back from 100…and sweet dreams. Take a deep breath," he said.

One deep breath and I smelled the root beer. The next thing I remember was waking up groggy in recovery. After a few hours, I was able to see the area on my body where the surgery was done. Dr. Templeton was considerate enough to cut over the same incision from previous surgeries. I would have less scaring and not be so self-conscious while in certain clothing and bathing suits, and I was grateful to have doctors that considered my "exterior" as well as my "interior."

Recovery was tedious, but I was determined. I was supposed to be in the hospital for about 10 days, but it dragged out to nearly 6 weeks. About one week after surgery, I dreamt that I pulled all of my IV's and tubing out and left the hospital to fly to Florida and see Sandra. But in my dream, she was gone from her hospital. She had died, and I sobbed for her when I woke up. This dream recurred so often that I began to share it with my parents and Dr. Templeton.

"I feel I need to hurry to her because she needs me in some way," I kept telling everyone. "Why does no one really hear what I am saying?"

After seeing how emotional I was, my parents finally told me the truth. "Sandra died. We, and your doctors, felt it best to wait to let you know. We all felt it would be best to let you recover somewhat before we broke something so terrible to you."

I needed to be sedated after I heard the news. "How could you not tell me?!" I cried. Our friendship was so strong that I believe I "felt" her death and then became deeply depressed. I could not eat, sleep came infrequently, and I felt that my recovery was deeply affected. It may have been part of the reason I remained in the hospital for 6 weeks instead of 10 days. Not being able to be a part of the funeral left me with no sense of closure.

Sandra's death pointed me in a new direction. After I left the hospital, I became mentally and emotionally stronger—realizing how fortunate I was to be alive. This new inner strength allowed me to see that I survived for a reason and she did not. I soon made a conscious decision that I was not going to remain a victim of my disease.

CHAPTER 22

I GIVE BACK

❧

I have often volunteered when the hospital asked me to visit children going through similar surgeries and experiences.

Through the years, I kept in touch with my doctors and with the hospital, as they obviously hold a very special place in my heart. I have often volunteered when the hospital asked me to visit children going through similar surgeries and experiences. Sometimes it was comforting for a sick child to see someone who had gone through a similar illness and survived. It renewed their hope.

The hospital called one particular time and asked me to visit a 14-year old-girl, Emily, who was extremely ill. "Would you have some time over the next week or so to visit Emily?" the secretary from Dr. Greenberg's office asked.

"Of course, I will find the time." I felt it was always important to visit prior to surgery so that they could see me as a healthy and perfectly normal adult.

As I dressed for the hospital visit, I was careful to choose clothing that disguised any evidence of my problem. I wanted those I visited to see that no one would know their business unless they chose to share it with them.

I took the train that morning from my house. As I sat, deep in thought, the hum of the engine relaxed me while I thought about my upcoming visit. I tried to think about what we would talk about. Would she even want to speak to me or would she want to be left alone. Before the 45 minute ride ended, I decided to be myself, to be honest and pleasant and let her lead the way.

When I arrived mid-morning at the hospital on that beautiful March day, I hoped I could share the warm spring weather with Emily. I walked into Children's Hospital thinking how odd it was being a visitor instead of a patient. I stopped at the desk to find out Emily's room number and rode the empty elevator to the adolescent unit on the 7th floor. I stopped outside the room to double check that I was in the right place and then slowly walked in. The room had four beds, and Emily was at the far side next to the windows.

She was lying in her bed and her mother was sitting off to the side. If they had not told me that Emily was 14, I would have figured her to be about 11. Her short brown hair covered her pale face, and she was so tiny that the bed seemed to consume her. An IV was all she was hooked up to since her surgery was not scheduled until the following day.

"How are you, Emily?" I asked quietly as I walked into her room.

"Who are you?" she wondered aloud. "Are you a nurse or a volunteer?"

"My name is Alesia," I answered, laughing at her comment. "I went through the surgery you are about to have when I was younger. The hospital staff felt it would be nice for us to meet and for you to see how normal you will be when this is all over."

Her dark eyes looked me over, uncertain as to how to react. She tried to sit up but I could tell she was very weak, and I was a little overwhelmed at her appearance. I never thought about how I looked to others when I was ill, but I paused to wonder before moving closer to the bed and sitting down on the other side of her mother.

"Wow, you are not what I expected when they told me you were coming. I am not sure what I did expect, but not someone cool like you." Her hands seemed so small when she ran her fingers through her hair, and I noticed how skeleton-like she looked. Her arms were as thick as toothpicks, and the bone structure in her face was hollow. Did I look like that back then?

Keeping my composure, I continued. "Thanks, Emily. I take a lot of pride in how I look, fitting in with my friends, and best of all, being healthy again. It is going to take a little time, but you will feel better every day. I will give you my phone number in case you want to ask me anything personal later, but is there anything you want to know now?"

She pondered this question. I knew that she and her mother would probably have a flood of questions, but at that moment, they were more concerned about getting through surgery. Emily began to cry a little, and her mother quickly reacted by sitting closer to the bed and holding her hand. I fully understood how Emily felt, both fear and relief, and how she was having difficulty expressing either.

"Why don't I just sit here for a while and tell you about me," I suggested. "I promise to try to visit when you are up and around after surgery. But for now, I just wanted to meet you and introduce myself, okay?"

Both Emily and her mom seemed relieved, and they relaxed while I told them about some of the time I spent at the very same hospital. I also shared with them my feelings about the place and about how I tried to visit people with problems similar to mine. I explained that I had a visitor who did the same for me after my surgery and how much it meant to me when I began to recover.

Emily continued to cry. "I am so scared to have an operation and wear a bag. It all seems so weird to me…but you look pretty normal," she said. "I cannot imagine life like that, but right now, I cannot imagine going on in this condition. Thanks for making the day before my surgery a little better for me," she said, cracking a frail smile.

I visited a few times and then got together with Emily during recovery. If there were any personal questions she felt comfortable enough to ask, I was there to answer them. When she asked to see my surgical area, I showed her. A master at hiding this bag, I dressed very fashionably at the same time to make all of the kids I visited comfortable.

Over the next couple of years, the hospital staff matched me up with three or four other people, but as medical science progressed, most patients underwent less radical surgeries than I had.

CHAPTER 23

MY NEW LIFE

I began to feel better and stronger and could concentrate on the fact that I was as close to normal as I was ever going to be.

When I returned from my 6-week stay in the hospital, the realization of not wearing a bag on my side any more finally hit me. I began to feel better and stronger and could concentrate on the fact that I was as close to normal as I was ever going to be. I was free of wearing a bag and now had to adjust to using a catheter daily and just covering the opening with a bandage. What a feeling of freedom for me not to have this thing hanging on my side. Still, I had to take special care of the surgery site, but compared to what I had to do before, this would be a breeze. A few obstacles deterred me along the way but eventually I became used to my new situation.

I began to eat normally again and engage in normal daily activities. Winter was coming to an end. I felt good and began to think about the coming summer—my first since childhood without a bag.

At 17, I began looking for a summer job in Brigantine—something different and fun that would allow me to spend the entire summer down by the shore. I was staying at a friend's summer home rent-free but still needed money to live on. A local pub known as the Boat Bar typically hired female bartenders, so I figured I had a good shot at a job there.

"Do you need any help here? I really need a job," I said to the gentleman behind the counter.

"As a matter of fact, we do need help. We're looking for a sandwich girl to help the barmaids with the lunch time crowd," he answered. His smile was nice and seemed sincere. He handed me an application, and I filled it out immediately. I was hired on the spot and began work the following day. Either he didn't notice my age on the application or conveniently overlooked it.

I liked the job—setting up the hot bar for all of the sandwiches. Better yet, I got to socialize all afternoon 4 to 5 days a week, so I really got to know people. One day, the manager came to me and said, "I am looking for another bartender, and I'm willing to train you. You seem reliable. Do you want to give it a try?"

Since I was already learning how to mix drinks by watching the bartenders day in and day out, I answered, "Sure! Why not?" The very next day, I was on the schedule.

I finished working one night, still in uniform but done for the evening, when the main boss—whom I hadn't really seen since my initial interview—came into the bar with friends. He was about 6 feet tall, with a medium build and slightly graying hair, probably in his mid 50s. Obviously, he had been drinking quite a bit, but I was polite and said hello. I headed to the ladies room before leaving, and suddenly felt him right behind me in the narrow hallway. He followed me right into the bathroom. I was stunned, frozen with fear. Pinning me up against the door so that no one else could get in, he tried to kiss me. His breath was stale and smelled of liquor.

"Are you nuts?" I screamed and pushed him away, knowing I needed to get away from him. "Please let me out!" I said sternly.

"Come on," he said. "Why not?" I shoved my way past him got the hell out of the bathroom. Running out of the restaurant, I fumbled my way into the car. Luckily, it was a short drive to my friend's house that night. When it was time for bed, I could barely sleep and tossed and turned all night, full of fear and humiliation. All I could do was lie there and think.

In my short lifetime, I had been through so much. Finally, I was healthy and strong and had control over my own life. I would not allow myself to be a victim any more, in ANY capacity. It was an overwhelming feeling to be treated this way. I could easily relate to a woman being abused by her boss and not being certain whether to say anything or not to anyone.

Ultimately, I decided not to share this experience with anyone. Since this was only a summer job, I could move on before anything else happened.

The next day, I came to work and put in my notice. I told my manager, the boss's niece, that I was unable to work there anymore but was afraid to say why.

"We are sorry you have to go, but we understand." She was very sweet.

Over the next two weeks, I worked there but did not charge one person for drinks. I consider myself honest—except for the age thing—but felt that the best way to punish this man was through his pocketbook.

CHAPTER 24

I MOVE OUT ON MY OWN

๑ ～ ๑

I was finally healthy, strong, and—for the first time—
liked something enough to want to learn more about it.

By the following summer, I had moved on and was working another summer job at the Chez, Atlantic City's most popular nightclub. I was 18 years old, sleeping all day in bed or on the beach and working all night. Being a bartender was like being the center of attention and every night was different—new faces, the latest music, and an exciting social scene. I was out and getting paid all at the same time!

Even though we were underage, Randee and I and some other friends managed to get into a lot of clubs, including the Chez. Sandra's sister Donna worked there, and our grief after Sandra's death brought us closer to her. When a job opened up, she got me in. I worked on Monday, Tuesdays, and Thursdays—days the regular bartenders did not want, but I did very well. I even decided to put college on hold until I figured out what I wanted to study.

Some of the craziest things happened in this place, which made it exciting to work there all night. Every shift was a new experience. Cliff, my boss, was easygoing and understood what people wanted when they stepped into a nightclub. He was a kind, quiet man with a knack for reading people's personalities immediately upon meeting them. He was about 5'9" with medium brown hair and a slightly stocky build. His face was gentle, but his way of observing people sometimes made him seem unapproachable. Some employees described him as scary, but I suspect his quiet nature put them off. In fact, he seemed so stoic that, as I got to know him better, I joined my coworkers in joking with him, telling him he seemed more like a boxer or a cop than a nightclub owner. We hit it off, and he and his father often visited me at work, stopping in for a few drinks after seeing live boxing matches in Atlantic City.

One night while Cliff stepped away from the bar to speak with an employee, his father Jack asked me, "What kind of relationship are you having with my son?"

Although I was surprised by this question, I was polite and respectful. "We are just friends, and I am a bartender here." Jack looked me straight in the eye and with all seriousness said, "Just keep it that way, and don't forget it. Understand?"

"Yep," I answered, unsure why he was so stern with me.

When I told Cliff about it, he explained that his father did not like Jewish people. In his day, you stayed with your own kind.

"He'll get over it," he said. "He did with my sister when she married a Jew." I wasn't quite sure what he meant by that, but I was intrigued. It was obvious to me that we liked each other, but we had only been social at work. Time will tell...I thought.

"I like this business," I said to Cliff one night when he came into the club. There was something that drew me to the atmosphere. At 18, I was too young to know exactly what it was, but something powerful had grabbed me. I was finally healthy, strong, and—for the first time—liked something enough to want to learn more about it. Even though I was only a bartender, I loved working every night, seeing new faces come and go, and getting to know our regular customers. I even dated a few of the regular guys, but nothing serious ever came of it. I was more interested in the business end of it: how things ticked day in and day out.

I began to wonder what happened between the closing in the wee hours of the morning until the doors were unlocked again at night. *How did everything get where it was supposed to be when we reported for work? Who cleaned the bathrooms, stocked the bars, and fixed the sound system?* I considered how much it cost to actually run the air conditioning and the light show, and to stock the bars with all those wonderfully expensive champagnes. It intrigued me how Cliff knew what music we should play and when, and how the lights worked in rhythm to the music. Who decided the format of the night and how do we know people will love it when they step into the doorway? As much as I wanted to ask these questions, I wasn't sure if they would sound ridiculous or if he would even understand my interest?

I told Cliff how I felt one night before we opened. "Oh yeah?" he said. "If you think you like this business so much, I'll show you the real business... if you're really serious," he added with a smirk that implied he had heard this sort of thing from employees before.

"Why do you sound so negative?" I asked.

"Everyone says that they like this business, but they don't know the blood and sweat that really goes into it. If you really think you like it, show up for work on Monday at noon."

Monday came, and I sat by the office waiting for him as he walked up the stairs. Judging by the surprised look on his face, he had not expected me to follow through.

"So, what brings you here?" he said, opening the office door.

"I came to learn the business, like you said...is that okay with you?" I said as I slowly followed him into the office.

"Okay," he said, "have a seat and let's get to work then."

Not sure what he expected of me, I sat and waited. In a few minutes, he handed me a big checkbook and a stack of bills. "We can share this desk since we don't have much room, okay?"

"Sure" I said. I got nervous immediately.

"What's wrong?" he asked.

I hesitated a moment and felt beads of sweat forming between my breasts. I took a deep breath and decided to come clean. If I was going to learn anything, I needed to be honest. "I don't know how to write a check," I told him.

If Cliff thought I was an idiot, he did a wonderful job of hiding it. He hesitated only a moment and then looked me in the eye. "Okay, give me the book back, come over to this side of the desk, and watch me."

After that, I realized how easy it was to keep a checkbook. At 18 years old, I had no reason to have ever written a check before then. I caught on quickly and became Cliff's assistant three days a week. We worked well

70

together, and I learned a lot just sitting there watching. By observing him, I noted his calm sense of order, conscientious organizational skills, and easy-going interactions with the staff. His mannerisms and gentle ways were stern enough to communicate who was the boss yet kind enough to motivate employees and business associates to do what he asked.

CHAPTER 25

NIGHTCLUB LIFE

∽

Dicey situations came with the night club business.
I was glad I had the perspective and guts to handle such times.

Some of the mob in Atlantic City and Philadelphia came in to the Chez to have a few drinks at times and never gave us a problem. One night, our friend and neighbor, Sue, was the cashier and her brother John was a doorman. Sue was a housewife and mother of two but was happy to be able to make a few extra dollars. It was around 4:00 a.m., and the club was packed. As always, the line was moving quickly, and Sue was collecting the cover charges from one person after another without ever looking up. "Five dollar cover charge," she said.

"What do you mean five dollar cover charge?" some guy asked.

"You heard me!" she answered sharply.

"I am not paying to get in here," the patron said loudly as he moved closer to her face. "Don't you know who I am? We don't ever pay to get in anywhere."

Sue stood up, got right back in his face, and again said, "Five dollar cover or you cannot get in, sir."

Her brother stepped in between them and told the guy to step away. "You heard what the lady said. Now pay the cover or get the hell out!" Obviously, John had no idea who he was dealing with either.

The guy turned around to leave with his buddies but not before threatening John. "I'm gonna blow you away for that," he said as he left.

At this point, no one cared who they were. But about fifteen minutes

72

later, the door opened, and the angry man pointed a gun at John, who was standing in the hall entrance.

"He's got a gun!" someone screamed.

The other doormen all ran into the building and slammed the door shut, bolted the lock, and stepped to the side. Sue grabbed the money in the drawer and ran to huddle together with the doormen. She and I, along with the door staff, were the only ones who realized what was happening. We called the police, but the guys took off before the police arrived.

The next day, some of their "people" contacted the club wanting to reach an "agreement" about what happened the night before. It seems that we had been extremely disrespectful to them by not recognizing them. However, the club managers smoothed it all over by explaining it was a simple mistake on the cashier's part, and no offense was intended. The mobsters seemed to understand that John was just protecting his sister, and the mob was willing to forgive and forget the "insult."

Another time, I was bartending upstairs on a Saturday night, and a very nice young couple came in for their usual weekend drinks. The man's name was John and he was the grandson of a mob guy from Philadelphia. I heard he was being groomed for a "top job" of some sort. The two sat down and ordered drinks and we kissed each other hello.

"How you guys doing?" I asked.

John's girlfriend Angela answered me but seemed out of sorts, "Okay, I guess," she answered.

Thinking I should leave them alone, I walked to the other side of the bar. As I turned around, they appeared to be arguing and then he stepped back and slapped her hard across the face. I was shocked.

"What the hell are you doing?" I said as I walked back.

"She was mouthing off to me," John said.

I was taken aback by what I had just seen. Angela sat there with her head down, holding her face, obviously embarrassed by the whole thing.

"I have the utmost respect for you both," I said, "and if she is going to let you slap her, that is her business. But if you hit her in front of me ever again, I will come over the bar and punch you myself. Do you understand?"

Of course, I quickly realized I probably overstepped my boundary, but the damage was already done. It was probably foolish of me to interfere, but I could not stand there and watch that kind of behavior.

Dicey situations came with the night club business. I was glad I had the perspective and guts to handle such times. One time, I decided to go to the club and hang out with my friends. Sitting alone at the bar, I stood up and leaned over to grab something. At that moment, some guy grabbed me from behind—between my legs—sticking his hand in my crotch. Quickly I turned around to see the guy and two doormen standing there. They grabbed the guy and said, "What the heck do you think you're doing?"

"She was asking for it," was his ridiculous reply.

"I just wanted to grab something behind the bar," I said. "What the hell are you talking about?"

"You were egging me on," he continued.

The doormen, knowing I would have never have done anything like that, grabbed the guy and tossed him out the door.

Needless to say, I learned to become very aware of my surroundings. The bar business taught me how to read people instantly. Early on, I learned the art of body language and non-verbal cues, communicating with my fellow employees about particular customers without anyone else knowing it. We created our own language about each customer, referring to them, what they drank or ate, and their bad or good habits.

The club was a melting pot and was never boring. Plenty of customers came and danced all night without spending any money at the bar, but they added to the atmosphere. They never gave us a hard time, so we would let them slide with no cover charge. The heavy spenders, the dancers, the mix of people, old, young, black, white, Hispanic, the amazing music, and the lights all contributed to the amazing success of the Chez. I learned more about business management by working in that bar than I could have from any college courses because I was smart enough to absorb everything Cliff wanted to teach me.

Randee and her soon to be husband Eric

Chelle (months old),
Alesia (4), and Jeff (8)

Chelle (4), Alesia (age 8), and Beepo

Cliff's parents Jack and Betty at their 50th
wedding anniversary

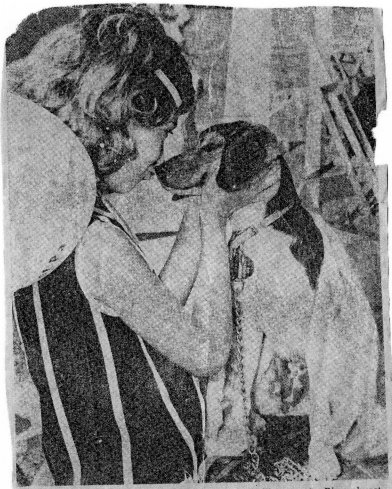

NOSE TO NOSE are Alesia Cohen, 9, of 1108 Wellington st., Rhawnhurst, and a canine entry in the Jeanes Hospital Fair Pet show. The fair started Friday evening and continued Saturday until 9 P. M. at the hospital

Alesia (9) with Beepo at the dog show

Alesia (17) at Childrens Hospital of
Philadelphia with singer Teddy Pendergras.

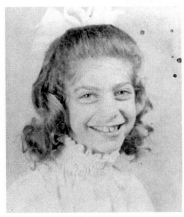

Alesia (9).

Sandra (high school, the year before
she was killed)

Cliffs sister Nancy, her husband Alan, and their
daughters Tracy and Hollie

My parents Evelyn and David

Cliff's family, Johnathan and me at Hollies 40th birthday (2005)

Sunset in Key West with our son and my cousin Laura (2000)

Me with Johnathan, My sister, Chelle with baby Corey, and My brother
Jeff with baby Michael.

Chelle, Laura and me at the Hard Rock Hotel during a
rare vacation together, 2006

Dr. C. Everett Koop

and the Session of Tenth Presbyterian Church

cordially invite you to attend the

Dedicatory Recital for the new

Elizabeth and David Koop Memorial Organ

to be played by Paul Jacobs

at the

Tenth Presbyterian Church

Seventeenth and Spruce Streets

Philadelphia, Pennsylvania

on

Friday, September 12, 2008

at 7:30 o'clock in the evening.

No admission charge. Free-will offering.

A rare invite ... Dr Koop invited me to a Church in
Philadelphia dedicating an organ in his wifes and sons
names both who have passed

December 5, 2007

Dear Alesia,

Whoever thought when I sat on your bedside and described an ileostomy to you that we'd still be corresponding when I'm ninety-two and you are a grandmother. I'm really not ninety-two, but I am in my ninety-second year, so that's the same thing.

I look forward to your annual letters-believe it or not-and I consider you to be one of my great accomplishments. I remember our talk about bikinis and ileostomies and high diving boards and all those things, and it has been a great joy to stand in the distance and watch you grow up and become a wife and a mother and all those other good things. Thank you for keeping me in your thoughts because I keep you in mine. It would be great if our paths could cross again sometime before I shuffle off. We'll see?

Sincerely,

C. Everett Koop, MD, ScD

One of many letters Dr Koop and I wrote
to each other over the years

82

January 6, 1997

Dear Alesia,

If I hadn't received a single other Christmas greeting this year, it would have been fine as long as I had yours. I don't imagine you know what it's like to look at you, grown up and beautiful, with such a lovely youngster and to know how close we came to losing you. You both are a joy to behold and I am so happy for all of you. This is one of the great joys of being a pediatric surgeon – you can see almost hopeless problems grow up into wonderful, productive people.

I wish you and yours all that is good in the new year.

Sincerely yours,

C. Everett Koop, M.D.

Another letter from Dr. Koop

The C. Everett
Koop Institute
at DARTMOUTH

C. Everett Koop, M.D., Sc.D.
Senior Scholar

January 2, 2004

Christmas wouldn't be the same if I didn't get a card from you. How many years has it been now? It is strange the way my mind works with old patients. I can see little vignettes of my relationships with you and specially remember the day we sat down and talked over what your operation would entail. It seems like just yesterday.

I'm on what I guess is my last project – putting my medical and public health lives on the Internet under a National Library of Medicine Website called, "Profiles in Science". It's about a three-year task for me, putting all television, documentaries, and lectures in suitable form. The big job is writing an introduction to each lecture from a perspective of twenty-five or more years later. However, it will be a rather unique archive, especially in reference to smoking and AIDS. My lectures alone fill over 200 volumes four inches thick – in big type to be sure.

Johnathan looks like a real boy; I hope he doesn't take that independent statement on his sweatshirt too seriously. Tell him he needs all the support he can get. I'm so pleased things have worked out so well for you. When I think of satisfactory patient experiences, you always come to mind at the top of the list. Take good care and have a wonderful New Year.

Sincerely yours,

C. Everett Koop/amb

C. Everett Koop, MD, ScD

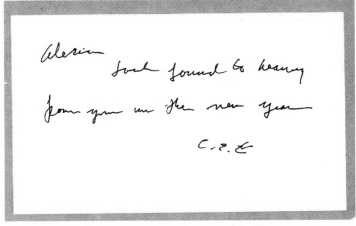

The last Holiday Note came by post card. Dr Koop
never forgot to keep in touch even when not well.

CHAPTER 26

TAKING SOME OWNERSHIP

*After much discussion, Cliff and I decided
to do the managing ourselves.*

Management problems at the bar grew worse. The bar business and nightlife are rough, especially when it is *all night*. A myriad of personalities, lack of sleep, drugs and alcohol, and the sheer craziness of the business managed to tire one of the managers, and he moved on. After much discussion, Cliff and I decided to do the managing ourselves. We had only been living together for several months, but Cliff had faith in me. We had a good working relationship and a solid system.

Our assistant manager, Donna, who had helped me get my first job, was in charge of Monday and Tuesday nights, which were typically slow nights.

"Donna, we need a boost on Monday nights," Cliff told her one evening when we were all in the office counting out for the night.

Donna looked up at Cliff. "Just for fun," she said, "let's throw a pajama party! We are in Casino City…we're the biggest and best club in town. Let's see if our customers are really paying attention."

Cliff didn't hesitate. "Do it and do it right," he said.

Everybody benefited when the club did well, so we liked all of the employees to get behind our promotions. We organized a strong campaign, complete with radio and newspaper ads, fliers, and plenty of good old fashioned word-of-mouth. Two weeks later, we were all dressed in our nighties, and so was every customer that walked through the door.

What a night! The club was packed with lingerie, footies, robes, cigars, pipes, and lots of alcohol. Everyone got into it, and we had an incredible Monday. At the end of the evening, I counted my tips and found it was the best night I'd ever had. I was addicted to the business.

One of our regulars and a big spender, Patricia, was older than I, about 30. She was nice—but aggressive. I heard she was into drugs and figured she was probably a dealer. Patricia stood about 5'6" with long blonde hair, and her extremely exaggerated makeup always included dark red lipstick. Her brash appearance alone made her stand out in a crowd, but her tone also demanded attention. She was always surrounded by a lot of people, and she paid their tab.

I was behind the bar that night and heard a big, "Hello, Alesia." It was Patricia. She wasn't wearing ordinary pajamas; she was head-to-toe slut in a red corset, fishnets, and very high heels. Her long boa draped over her corset, and when she moved it aside, her breasts were practically falling out of her outfit. By today's standards, she would have been right at home, but in the early 80s, her image really turned some heads.

"Hello there! You look...shall I say, great!" We both laughed. I served her drinks throughout the night, as well as the many people surrounding her. I suspected they were high on more than just alcohol but didn't share my observations with anyone else. Patricia and her entourage added a lot of "color" to the evening, but I never saw her again after that. She simply disappeared. People come and go in this business. Still, I wondered what happened to her.

One day, a few weeks after that party, someone told me she heard that Patricia had overdosed after she and some friends spent an entire weekend in her apartment doing drugs. Patricia never came out of her bedroom the entire weekend, and she was found dead on Sunday.

The moment I heard this, I recalled a neighbor who died while away at college. It was someone from the neighborhood who was a few years older than I was and friendly with my older brother. Apparently, not long after he arrived at school he died from a fall over a balcony—he was either thrown or was so stoned that he fell. When his room was searched, a guitar case filled with drugs was found. His parents never accepted his passing, but the senselessness of it came flooding back to me when I heard about Patricia. I actually had known two people who had died from drugs by the time I turned 20 years old.

CHAPTER 27

WORKING IN A NIGHTCLUB!

Security tried their best to control the environment,
but nightclub life can be a breeding ground for abuse unless
you keep your head on straight.

Working in a hot ("hot" meaning busy and popular!) nightclub has its ups and downs. It was very difficult to date anyone who understood that you had to flirt and dress sexy as part of the job. Cliff and I had a good working relationship from the beginning. When I worked behind the bar, I was a bartender, making money for the club and for myself. Other times I helped manage the building and staff, making the customers feel welcome. The same went for Cliff. Together, we both did what we were there to do.

Since we were the biggest and the best club around, finding men was not a problem. I dated a few different guys briefly but nothing too serious. It didn't take long before I had heard every line. I quickly learned that the bar business and steady relationships with customers didn't work. The problem was that when I stopped seeing someone, I didn't necessarily stop seeing them. If they kept coming in, there wasn't much I could do about it.

One of my coworkers, Joanne, had recently broken up with a guy she had dated for a few months. The following weekend while she and I were behind the bar working, her former boyfriend walked in and sat at her side of the bar with another woman. Joanne needed to keep her composure since we always tried to remain professional, keep our mouths shut, and be courteous to customers. This guy began kissing and playing around with his new date, obviously to upset Joanne. As the night progressed, things got even uglier. The more the couple drank, the more intimate they became, and the more upset Joanne got. Finally, she couldn't take any more. She stormed out from behind the bar, punched her ex in the face, and headed to the office to calm down. The guy was pissed but continued to come in every week with different women until—after awhile, it stopped mattering. All of us girls at the Chez had similar stories about guys like that, and we all grew wiser.

Through it all, I managed to keep myself very grounded. When these kinds of things happened, I told my co-workers, "I need to stay focused and keep remembering why I am here. I need to make money, for one thing, and if these guys choose to act like asses after we end a relationship, then so be it." I wanted more out of life, and this stuff seemed minor to me in comparison to what I had been through.

Another problem in the club was that drugs were plentiful. Security tried their best to control the environment, but nightclub life can be a breeding ground for abuse unless you keep your head on straight. About half of the Chez employees and customers managed to get caught up in the "scene." It usually began with a little experimenting and eventually became part of everyday life.

Cocaine, Quaaludes, and crystal meth were popular during those years, and some people mixed their drugs with booze. The drug of choice in my younger years was either cocaine or meth. I experimented very little and immediately found out that I did not want to stay up for days at a time. After a few experiences, I decided not to bother and quietly moved on. Most of the people that partied together split into 50/50 groups. Fifty percent of us got it together and became successful and the other fifty percent remained in the same partying mode for years and became stagnant in their lives. They are still in some cases—working, spending all of their money on drugs, and not going anywhere in life.

Strangely enough, even the Atlantic City street pimps came in once in a while for drinks with friends after work. Sometimes they brought their girls, but usually it was just the guys. It was all I could do to keep from laughing at their crazy clothing and hats.

After a few drinks, they would continuously offer me "extra work" and I would say, "No thanks. Not my style, but I appreciate you asking." They got a kick out of me for some reason, and all of the guys brought me small gifts on the holidays. I always thought it was because I did not mistreat them or ask them to leave. Truth is, they were a nice addition to our mix of colorful clientele.

One of them became a regular customer. He was very dark skinned, about 6' 2", and always wore a cowboy hat with a sports jacket. I mixed his drinks while he tried to pick me up.

"Hey Joe," I would wave him over toward me. "What's happening."

Joe gave me a big smile, and looked me "up and down" as if he was trying to see through me. Leaning on the bar with one elbow, he kissed my cheek, and said, "Nothing baby, until I saw you tonight."

I smiled, mixed his drink, and joked around with him for a few minutes if I wasn't busy. Our conversations were far from serious or important, but he came to visit often. Joe even brought me a Ralph Lauren cowboy hat for Christmas one year; I kept it for years.

One of my favorite bartending partners (and the most amazing bartender I have ever seen), became a lifelong friend. Eddie had a remarkable memory for names, drinks, and faces. He mixed your usual drink, shook your hand, and lit your cigarette in the time it took you to pull out a barstool. After years of working together, Cliff gave Eddie an opportunity to become a partner in the business and give up bartending. Eddie took the chance, made an investment with us, and we have been together ever since.

CHAPTER 28

CLIFF

*Cliff liked the finer things in life but worked hard for them,
which I liked and respected.*

Cliff loved sports and talked to me about it whenever we were together. I, on the other hand was not sports oriented at all. I enjoyed coming to work every day and tried to find something about sports to talk about. I looked forward to seeing him and grew to like him a bit more every time I saw him. Then I had the idea to read the headlines of the sports section every day before work. If I just mentioned the headline, he would chime in and finish the conversation. He was thrilled to have someone to talk to at work about sports and our fondness for each other began to grow.

One day, Cliff asked me if I wanted to go out for a drink after work. "Of course, that would be nice," I said. I thought nothing of going out after work with my boss for a cocktail, since he was living with his girlfriend at the time, and I was dating someone as well. We headed to the Sands Casino about one block away, so we could leave our cars and relax for a while.

We stepped into the casino, headed toward the bar in the center of the room, ordered drinks, and began talking shop. He told me he was impressed with my eagerness to learn and said how nice it was to have help during the day. Our conversation came easily, and the hour flew by before we both had to go. We left for the evening and went our separate ways.

It slowly became a habit for Cliff and I to go out for a drink after work. One day he confessed that he was unhappy with his girlfriend and was breaking up with her, saying the relationship had been over for a long time. He added that I was the reason he was asking her to leave.

We kept it platonic for a long time until we both were free of other relationships.

Not long after I broke up with the person I was seeing, Cliff asked me to go to New York for a few days. We packed a few things, took a couple days off, and went to New York. We checked into the Pierre Hotel across from Central Park. Staying at the Pierre showed me how the "other half lived" in the city that never sleeps. We stepped into the lobby, and I could feel the "old money" as we headed toward the front desk. When we got into the elevator to go to our room, the operator actually bowed his head when I stepped in. The bellhop did the same thing when I walked into our room. It struck me as weird to have people bowing to me...but it was kind of cool, too!

The room was not overdone, not too large, and was decorated so beautifully that it took my breath away. I may have only been 20 years old at the time, but I immediately knew I could easily adjust to the finer things in life. Our room had a tastefully decorated living room and a large master bedroom with a bath. It was the first time I had ever been in a hotel room this large. I knew that Cliff was about to wine and dine me in a new world, and I immediately wanted more.

After our return, Cliff arrived at the club one night and said, "Go upstairs and look in the desk drawer on the right. There is a surprise for you."

I quickly scurried upstairs, unlocked the office door, and sat down at the desk. Although my hands were shaking and my heart beating rapidly with excitement, I took a deep breath and opened the desk drawer. Inside was a small box wrapped with light pink paper. I quickly opened the gift, tearing the paper off and tossing it into the trashcan by the desk. Inside the box lay a beautiful solid gold whistle. The card that lay next to it read, "If you ever need me, just whistle. Love, Cliff." Oh my god, I thought, how sweet and kind of him.

I ran down the stairs quickly with the whistle in my hand, went right up to Cliff, and placed a long kiss on his lips. Although people had figured out we were dating, we kept displays of affection completely private up to that point. We looked up to see everyone's shocked faces, but the staff quickly went on with whatever business they had been tending to.

That night when I got home to my apartment, I was still excited and could not wait to tell my roommate Barbara about my gift. The outcome of our conversation, however, was not what I expected. She thought Cliff was using me and told me not to see him any more since I would only end up being hurt. My initial feeling was that if I needed motherly advice, I would have called my own mother. I wanted my girlfriend to be happy that I was beginning a new and exciting relationship with someone who seemed to care for me. What was wrong with her?

Christmas came that year, and Cliff bought me a beautiful Orfers crystal horse's head for my apartment that weighed about 25 pounds. It looked beautiful in my bedroom, and I thought of Cliff any time I looked at it.

Not long afterward, we decided to move in together. It would be the first time I would live with a boyfriend. He understood of my nervousness and helped me pack my things and move in. That evening, we were enjoying the night lying on the couches and watching television when I suddenly noticed a beautiful larger version of my horse's head in the living room.

"Cliff, where did that beautiful horse's head come from?" I asked.

Cliff laughed. "I knew when I gave that small crystal horse head to you, it would someday sit with the larger one I had here." Now that freaked me out—in a good way!

I had met the person I was meant to be with. Our age difference was about 19 years but it felt irrelevant. His considerate and gentle way, his drive toward business, and his kindness drew me closer. He gave me plenty of room to make my own decisions and mistakes, offering advice only when I asked. Cliff liked the finer things in life but worked hard for them, which I liked and respected. He was headed in the direction I wanted to be going, too. I was going to stay.

CHAPTER 29

LET'S BUY ANOTHER BUSINESS

*Within several months, we were the biggest hit from
Atlantic City to Philadelphia.*

When Cliff and I had been dating for about a year, he decided to buy the club next door to the Chez as an investment. Doing so meant that he controlled a street-to-street property in the ever-growing casino town. That is, the new club was on a wide property with access to it from two parallel streets. Investing in that kind of desirable property was a wise real estate strategy.

The building was in sad shape, but we still went through with the deal. Not wanting to compete with the Chez, we decided to transform the new property into a gay nightclub—the biggest and nicest of its kind in Atlantic City. Originally called "The Saratoga," we liked the name and decided not to change it.

We lived about 30 miles outside of Atlantic City in an area that was perfect for raising a family. As luck would have it, we also owned approximately eleven acres across from our home that was a cedar forest. "If milled properly," Cliff said, "that wood will be perfect for the renovation of our new nightclub. Let's bring out the staff, and we'll chop the trees down and make a deal with the local mill to make wood for the walls. It will not only be beautiful, but we will have done all the work ourselves."

I thought this was ingenious but impossible, but I went along with Cliff's idea, which unfolded into a wonderful and rewarding project. Most of the staff helped with the task and together, we all nailed up and stained the wood. We transformed a 6,000 square foot building into the most beautiful club I had ever seen.

When you walked through the wooden fence, you went through our private deck and restaurant, toward the entrance. Upon paying the cover charge, you walked into a room that had soundproof doors that—when closed—allowed you to drink and socialize with only background music. Through the doorways, you stepped into a room with two bars and an over-sized, elevated dance floor with a state of the art light show. The place felt comfortable with an island-y look, from the wood on the walls to the "tropical" bartender uniforms.

Within several months, we were the biggest hit from Atlantic City to Philadelphia. Gay and straight people from all over, including our nightclub next door, came to "see and be seen" at Club Saratoga. You could sit outside on the deck and sip a cocktail or go into the dancing section and have the time of your life. From drag shows to luaus...whatever the event, everyone came dressed in costume.

Our theme parties were a blast, and people waited in line to come in and see new faces nightly. Every little detail of every party was considered, from the type of food served at the luau to the crowning of the king and queen at a prom. Halloween was also a big event for us. The show LaCage ran in the casinos for years, and we were lucky enough to have the entire cast come dressed at different times for all of our events as well.

On our first New Years Eve, the excitement was overwhelming. We hoped to have our biggest night of the year. It seemed as if our wishes would come true when the phone rang at the Chez. I happened to be in the office and picked up the phone to hear Cliff on the other end, calling from the Saratoga.

"Alesia, come down here right away," he said sternly.

I knew something was wrong but figured Cliff just needed someone to vent to. I hung up and took off. The Chez was full to capacity, and the line was down the street, but the staff had everything under control.

I rushed down the street and straight into the office at the Saratoga, where I found Cliff and both managers.

"I just counted and wrapped $10,000, closed the safe, clicked it shut, and stepped out of the office for a few minutes. When I returned and re-opened the safe to make change, the money was gone," he explained hysterically. I'd never seen him like that before, standing there yelling and looking at no one in particular. It was scary.

Donna, our manager at the time, tried to clarify things. "I was in the back of the club and happened to walk in to the office right when Cliff got here."

Donald, our assistant manager, had been at the Chez greeting customers and was with me when I entered the Saratoga. Now, we all stood together in shock.

"We started searching customers' bags before we even called you," Cliff continued. "But I don't know how they could have gotten into the office. It doesn't make sense! We even climbed on chairs and checked the drop ceilings in case someone threw it up there to come back later for it." Probably, it had happened too quickly for the thief to be one of the customers; that left it an inside job.

I was shocked and couldn't even speak. I tried to process what he was telling me in the few minutes I was there. I wondered how and when the money disappeared, and where it could be. The rest of the New Year's party was spent searching and trying to get to the end of the night without losing our minds or upsetting customers.

At the end of the evening, everyone who worked for us stayed, despite the fact that they were tired. They were searched, questioned, and then sent home late that morning, knowing they were suspects. Even though they were all busy, someone knew our routine and managed to steal the money. Everyone took a lie detector test, and while one person's results were inconclusive, there was never any solid evidence. We lost a lot of money on our first big holiday in business but knew "the show must go on." I felt sad about going to work day after day, knowing that there was a good chance one of our colleagues had betrayed us. Something forever changed in me that day.

After months of investigating, the police and detectives came up empty handed. It was dramatic for us to go through this and still move on, but we managed to keep calm during the ordeal. If we wanted to succeed—and we did—we had no choice but to put the past behind us. We still had a business to run. Our one-year anniversary was rapidly approaching, and we had a lot of planning to do to pull off a party worthy of the Saratoga. Food, strippers, and great music were all part of the agenda for the evening, and everyone came to celebrate with us.

Every night in a gay club is an event, with or without a theme party. There were nightly drag queens dressed to the nine's, and there was a beautiful person always looking for another beautiful person. All those beautiful people flowed through the doors that night.

A memorable moment that evening was when Whaylon Flowers, a casino entertainer who has since passed away, brought in his puppet "Madam." He was a wonderful person, very warm and friendly—and entertaining because he always included his puppet when he spoke to you. Whaylon and "Madam" were a couple, and even after he was intoxicated, the puppet still remained in the conversation!

One night, a guy came in who was so drunk that we refused to let him stay. We turned him away and figured that was that. Needless to say, during the strip show, everyone's attention was on the stage. Out of nowhere, a ceiling tile suddenly hit a customer in the head—followed by a body. From the waist down, this guy was hanging from the ceiling, but the emcee for the strip show never missed a beat.

"Put the spot light on this surprise that Cliff has planned for us!" he joked. Everyone focused on the guy hanging from the ceiling, and the show kind of stopped. But the emcee knew that Cliff had a taste for the element of surprise, so he assumed it was part of the night's events and had everyone cheering.

Cliff and I ran over to the area and looked up. When the DJ turned the music down, we heard the guy screaming for help, but he was also screaming for someone to get him another beer. A doorman brought a ladder to try to help, but we finally had to call the fire department to rescue the guy. When they arrived, they demanded that the lights be turned on and that everyone leave the building.

"I certainly will not empty the building during this party!" Cliff yelled at the fire chief. "Get this freakin guy out of here now!" By that time, the police were there as well.

"We cannot take him down with everyone here," said the chief.

At that moment, the entire room of about 500 people started screaming at the police, saying they would wait for them to get him out but would not move from the building.

"Okay," the chief conceded, obviously outnumbered. "Have it your way."

About half an hour went by before they managed to get him cut down from the ceiling, but the duct work was stuck on him like a girdle. They handcuffed him, duct work and all, and took him to the police station.

On the way out the guy yelled, "I told you I could not be kept out!"

It was then that the doorman recognized him as the drunk guy he'd turned away earlier that evening. We figured out that he must have gone behind the building, climbed up the rain spout, got on the roof, and come in through the air conditioning system. He really had to work to get in to the club!

After the police and firemen left, the lights went back off, the music came on, and the party continued. The damage to the building was major—the entire air conditioning system had to be redone—but we all had something to talk about for a long time after that.

CHAPTER 30

MEETING KERRY

How would she like me?

The crazy night scene was the professional side of our life. On the personal side was a slowly but steadily growing family life. Cliff had a 7-year-old daughter. Not wanting to force a meeting too soon, we waited two or three months until we knew that things were solid enough to bring Kerry and I together.

When Cliff asked if I was ready to meet her, I immediately replied, "Of course I am!" but I was secretly nervous that he already had a child. How would she like me?

"I will invite her and one of her friends over for the weekend, so that the girls will have each other to play with," he suggested.

I was waiting by the door when they arrived that Friday afternoon after school. Both girls were cute and loved to play together. Cliff introduced us, and the girls went to Kerry's bedroom to play.

Cliff asked, "Well, what do you think?"

"Kerry seems a bit shy, but I think we will get along just fine. She seems like a great kid."

I headed to the bedroom to play with them and see if I could get them to talk to me a little. Before I knew it, we were sacked out on the beds in Kerry's room, and she was staring at me smiling. "So what is fun to do around here?" I asked them.

"Well, Barbies are our favorite thing to do, and we love to color and dress up," Jennie answered. It seemed Kerry was the quiet one, and Jenny spoke for them both.

After a few minutes, Jenny looked me right in the eye and asked, "So, are you going to be the new mother here?" I looked at her, shocked by the question, because she was so young to ask something like that. Kerry began laughing right away. I hesitated for a moment, and thought honesty was the way to go with kids.

"I guess I am," I said. I was also laughing with them, more out of nervousness, but that seemed to break the ice. From then on, Kerry and I bonded. I assume she trusted me right away because I was honest and didn't dance around the bold question. She visited us every other weekend after that, and although things were rocky with Cliff and his ex-wife, we always kept Kerry (and me) out of their differences. After awhile, we decided a family trip to Bush Gardens in Virginia would be nice. We packed up both girls—bold Jenny and quiet Kerry—their Cabbage Patch dolls, and way too many suitcases (since the dolls needed clothes, too!) and left for Virginia. Six hours later, we checked into the hotel, which was like a little apartment, and showed the girls their bedroom. As we were leaving to go to dinner, Kerry began to cry, saying she wanted her mommy.

"I want to see her now," she sobbed, as Cliff and I looked at each other and realized that she had never been this far away from her mom.

"Okay, let's give her a call, Ker," he said as she held onto him, crying.

Her mom answered the phone and did a good job of calming Kerry down. But within minutes, Jenny was crying and saying she needed her mom, too. We called her mother, she calmed down, we went to dinner, and the rest of the trip was so much fun. Neither girl had time to worry about their mother.

We took the girls to the park daily, then to fancy restaurants every night. We dressed up and did our hair together, and I helped them dress when they needed it. We swam in the hotel pool, played games, and won prizes. One day in the park, the girls insisted on playing a ring toss game with extra large prizes. Cliff told them that if they won anything too big, they could not take it home. I interrupted and said, "I think that if we win big stuffed animals, we'll manage to squeeze them into the car for the ride home!" They begged and pleaded with Cliff to let us play, and he finally gave in. With my help, we won two prizes—stuffed animals that were bigger than the girls. We had to follow through with the promise of finding room in the car for the animals. Cliff was sure it would not work, but even with the two girls, their toys, and two oversized stuffed animals squeezed into the backseat for a six-hour ride home, we did not hear a single complaint out of anyone the entire way home.

CHAPTER 31

I MEET THE REST OF THE FAMILY

*Once both families realized that we were serious about our relationship
—and we were going to move forward with or without them—
they slowly came around.*

When we decided to move in together, Cliff told his family about his recent breakup and said that he and I would be living together from now on. He spoke to his sister on the phone and tried to explain how unhappy he had been with his girlfriend, Ellen, who he had lived with for a few years. His sister Nancy had grown very close to Ellen and seemed to be having a hard time with the breakup—and with me. Part of the problem was that both of Nancy's daughters were about my age, so I could understand there would be some discomfort. There was a 19-year age difference between Cliff and me, so I understood his sister struggling with the idea.

Cliff and I were talking one day when Cliff again tried to explain his reasons for the breakup with Ellen. "I know we have spoken about this before," he began. "Ellen had a serious drug and alcohol problem for a long time. I just could not deal with it anymore and do hope that you and my family understand the reasons for my decisions." Cliff continued as if he felt he again owed me this explanation. "I slowly realized how unhealthy this relationship was for me and that it was not headed in a positive direction."

"Okay," was all I could say. I figured time would allow whatever was going to happen, to happen. It did not take long for the shit to hit the fan.

The phone rang at our home, and Cliff answered to find Nancy on the end of the line planning a family barbeque. I could only hear Cliff speaking, but it did not sound good. "No, Nan, I will not be able to come tomorrow. You did what? Why would you do that? No, if you are not going to invite Alesia, who is my new girlfriend to your home, then don't call and invite me anymore either!" he told her in a bitter tone of voice. As he hung up, he turned to me and told me that I was not welcome in her home and she had invited Ellen.

Cliff only had one sister, and although I understood that his ex-girlfriend was part of the family for a few years, I was hurt and unsure how I would deal with the situation. I showed no emotion at that time; I felt Cliff was feeling bad enough. Instead, I spent a few days wrestling with my feelings and knew he would somehow handle the situation. It was best for me to remain quiet.

It was a while before he heard from Nancy again, but eventually she called and invited us both over for a dinner. I went and was very polite to his sister and her husband. It was a little strained throughout the evening, however. I assumed after a while that Nancy would take seriously what Cliff had said to her: "Ellen is gone and Alesia is here to stay, whether you like it or not."

I planned to remain quiet with his nieces, too. Since both girls were right around my age, I thought I could manage a friendship over time with them. They had also grown close to Ellen, but I hoped that everyone would recover, move on, and include me as family eventually.

Tracy, Nancy's oldest daughter, was nice to me but spent a lot of time getting together with Ellen in the beginning. Hollie, who at the time was around 15 years old, was still in high school and was extremely active in sports like diving, softball and golf. It didn't take me long to see that she loved life and people and embraced everything with a passion. We clicked immediately. She was also quite close with Ellen but was able to find room for me right away. Being close in age helped us to find things in common.

Both the girls and their mother struggled with the big age difference between Cliff and me. But I was sure of myself and knew that this relationship was what I wanted.

Still, there were things we needed to talk about. Cliff and I spoke about our age difference often.

"I am concerned that our ages are going to make a big difference as our lives continue," Cliff expressed to me one day. I was understanding of his concerns and had a few of my own, but we cared for one another and seemed very compatible in many ways.

"I think this is something we can both conquer over time," I would tell him. Sometimes when you try to follow the rules too closely, you falter." We were not about to let "rules" get in the way of things, so we both agreed to move forward and give it some time.

My parents did not want to like Cliff because of our age difference, but they were willing to have lunch and at least meet him. Almost immediately, my mother hit it off with him, and slowly my dad warmed up, too. Conversation was light, and Cliff's easy manners and sense of humor won them both over by the end of the meal.

Chelle, who was a teenager at the time, liked Cliff right away. We went to visit her and my parents often and then invited them for a visit at our house.

Over time, the age difference mattered less and less. Once both families realized that we were serious about our relationship—and we were going to move forward with or without them—they slowly came around. Later Cliff's family admitted that he had made the right decision by ending his relationship with Ellen, saying that she was truly messed up on drugs and alcohol, and that she had created a very unhealthy environment for him as well as herself.

Nancy, her daughters, and I grew fond of one another over the years, it seems we were always close.

My family grew to love Cliff. In fact, the family joke soon became, "If Cliff and Alesia end up getting a divorce, the family will take Cliff and leave Alesia!"

CHAPTER 32

THE WEDDING

*I am really engaged! was all I could say
every time I looked at my finger.*

I knew I did not want to do the traditional wedding, and I got my wish! True to form for us, even our engagement was out of the ordinary. Out of the blue one day, Cliff showed me the most beautiful diamond ring. It was in a man's setting.

"What do you think?" he asked. I loved it! Toying with it in his hand, he said, "This diamond was something I purchased many years ago as an investment, and I have decided this is the diamond we will have set for our engagement."

By the time I picked out the setting at the jewelers, I was feeling a sense of excitement that caught me by surprise. I had never planned to get married at a young age—certainly not at 20 years old. The engagement ring was beautiful, and I wanted to keep it on my hand. Still, I decided to hand it back to Cliff until we both felt ready. I even knew where he kept it but tried not to think about it. I would often pass by his hiding place and think about how beautiful the ring was. Someday I would have it on my hand all the time. How would it feel? When was he going to give it to me? I would sometimes wait until I was home alone, sneak over and put it on to admire how beautiful it looked. I would slip it on my finger and stare at it for a while. Then very carefully, I put it back exactly where Cliff left it so he wouldn't know I even knew where it was.

As I approached my 21st birthday, I recalled something Cliff and I laughed about from time to time. Because we met when I was 18 and fell in love when I was 19, Cliff used to joke that he wouldn't marry me until my age started with a 2. Well, the next thing I knew, I was walking into a wonderful surprise 21st birthday party on the deck of our gay nightclub. All my friends, family, and some employees were there on a warm September evening. Although I was a little taken aback by the whole thing, I just went with the flow of it, even when they sat me on a chair and asked me to open my gifts in front of everybody. As I was opening the last gift, I saw Cliff come across the deck with a small box in his hand. I was the only one in the room who knew what was in the box. Our eyes met and locked. He handed the box to me, and the room was quiet. I took it from him, began to cry, and walked out of the party, overwhelmed and shocked.

A few of my friends followed me inside the building—along with Cliff.

"How could you do this to me?" I cried.

"Do what?" he asked.

"Give me this ring in front of everyone," I was crying. "You were supposed to give this to me one night while we were alone, drinking champagne, dining…with you down on one knee."

"I was?" Cliff was flabbergasted.

"I don't know, I just thought that was what you would do," I kept crying.

In the meantime, I opened the box and put the ring on, forgetting I had just walked out on an entire party. I wiped my eyes, regained my composure, and walked back outside. Everyone looked up and got quiet, not knowing what to expect at that moment. I held out my hand and cried, "We're getting married!"

Everyone went crazy and yelled and applauded. I was embarrassed by my reaction. I apologized but everyone seemed too excited to care. Some people said that they thought we had had an argument or something. The rest of the evening went fine, and I felt better as the night wore on.

When Cliff and I were alone for a few minutes in the office before the end of the party, I threw my arms around him and gave him a long soft kiss. We looked each other in the eyes and smiled, it was just a moment but it managed to relax us both and reassure me that everything was fine and it was kind of silly to react the way I had earlier. The rest of the night, I kept staring at my finger, the beauty of my new engagement ring and the warmth I felt inside was surreal.

I am really engaged! was all I could say every time I looked at my finger. My mind was rushing a mile a minute. Was I truly ready to plan a wedding? My wedding? I never put any thought into my wedding, a dress, or walking down the aisle because I planned to go to college, marry in my thirties, and maybe have two children. Most of my girlfriends had their dresses picked out when we were teens, but I had no time for that—never truly believing I would marry young. Now 21 years old, I was faced with all of these mind boggling questions.

"Honey, I was married once before and did the whole wedding thing, so I would prefer not to do that again," Cliff said.

"I'm thrilled you feel that way because I don't think I would make it down the aisle if we did the traditional thing," I told him, thinking I would chicken out halfway down and turn around and leave. I do not know why I thought that way, I just did. "I'd be glad to do something different," I told him and saw the relief on his face.

"Let's go to Key West and spend the same amount of money that a wedding might cost, but do it in a different way," he said, obviously inspired.

"Sounds like a plan," I answered without hesitation.

I chose to cook Thanksgiving dinner. Our house was the largest at the time, and we could have both families together for the first time. During dinner, we announced to the families what we had decided and told them that anyone who cared to join us was welcome. We intended to go away and be on our honeymoon already when we "tied the knot."

Everyone got quiet at the table and after a few minutes, they began to share their thoughts. My mother said, "Just give us the information and we will be there, but we still want you to have some kind of wedding for our friends and all the family."

Cliff and I looked at each other, and I spoke out first. "Well, we could throw a party at the club because the reason we are going away is to stay away from the traditional wedding."

Cliff then joined in and said, "You could throw a party at the club and invite everyone we know. If we use the club and all help, we could save

107

money and still invite everyone. How does that sound?"

I liked the idea, and the entire family chimed in with their thoughts and opinions. We all just wanted a party of some kind to celebrate. My parents now had something to plan. My mother was incredibly excited, but I was dreading what she had in store for me.

Between Thanksgiving and the wedding date—February 10—we had about 10 weeks to plan. We took a trip to Key West by car immediately after New Years to have blood work done, find someone to marry us, and arrange hotel rooms for us and those that were joining us. The trip was relaxing and rewarding once we got the planning done. Trying to keep things as simple as possible became a challenge, but we conquered it. We were lucky enough to have friends that lived in Key West who helped us find the right people we needed to make our plans come to fruition.

In February of 1983, we drove to Key West for the real thing—the wedding. The drive took about 24 hours, which we normally broke up into two or three days. We contacted a former employee who had moved to Georgia and arranged for a visit and an overnight stay. That was a nice break from the road trip, and we dined and went to the grand opening of a new nightclub with him during our visit.

We arrived at the Pier House Hotel as scheduled. As we were checking in, the manager of the hotel made a deal to let us use the Sunset Suite for our entire 12-day stay instead of our planned few days after the wedding. The suite was beautiful, with a perfect view of the Atlantic Ocean from the balconies, which were the highest in the entire hotel. It was the size of a condominium with a full kitchen, bar, and living area—perfect for a party, especially a wedding.

Our wedding day could not have been more beautiful. At least 20 people flew in the night before. They were all sunning when Cliff headed to the airport to pick up my parents, sister, brother, and brother's wife.

Then, as they were checking into the hotel, the sky got dark. This was very unusual for Key West, and we all scrambled. One minute, the day was perfect. The next, the sky opened up and the rain began. It came on so suddenly that while we were running to the rooms I thought that it would pass quickly, like most afternoon storms in Florida. We still had time; sunset was not until 6:00 p.m. this time of year and it was only 3:30.

Back at the room, I showered and passed the time playing with my hair, watching television, and staring at the rain. After about an hour, it began to dawn on me that the rain might not stop.

How am I going to get out of the room, across the hotel? Will I have to stand out in the rain to get married? What are we going to do? I began to feel over-whelmed.

Cliff watched the weather and decided that we were not leaving the suite to do anything, let alone get married. He approached me in the bedroom while I stared out the windows, looking for a break in the sky.

"Alesia, we need to rethink this very quickly. We are getting married in about 1 ½ hours, and it is not going to happen outside. It's too late to put something together with the hotel; we have lots of booze, lots of food, and lots of space right here in our room. We need to call everyone and have them meet up here."

I hesitated and then realized he was not kidding. "There goes my sunset wedding dream, huh?" I said. "Well, at least we have this great room, enough space for lots of guests, right?"

The Key West friends who had helped us came early to assist in arranging the room. They told me not to worry about anything, and that I should go get dressed. It rained so hard that we could not even leave our suite. I still am not sure how people got to our room without arriving fully drenched. It felt like a hurricane with strong winds and heavy showers.

In preparation for the event, my parents brought an extra suitcase filled with food from Philadelphia.

"What's in the suitcase?" I asked as they placed it on the kitchen table.

"Food for the wedding," my father said as if he always carried around a suitcase full of food for any given occasion!

Cliff and I looked at each other, trying not to have any reaction as the suitcase clicked open. My father began to show us everything he brought.

"Real Jewish corned beef, pastrami, smoked fish, all kinds of cheese, knishes… We will eat like kings tonight," he said to Cliff. I had heard him say that often during my childhood when he was bubbling over with pride.

I was not sure whether to be embarrassed or whether to laugh, but I made light of it even though I wanted to die. All I could think when I looked at Cliff was that the poor guy was going to marry into a family of nuts. Cliff, on the other hand, did not seem to be upset and told my dad he would be back shortly. He wanted to pick some things up to complete the meal.

A bit later, Cliff came back and handed a big bag to my girlfriend, Terry, who had come to help lay out the food before the guests arrived. She opened the bag and said, "Oh great! Shrimp! Everyone will go crazy!" In her next breath, she looked at me and said, "What do we do with these? They still have their heads on."

At that point, I was ready to kill both my father and my future husband. Terry spent most of the evening peeling heads off shrimp and making faces at me. Cliff's reaction was quite innocent. "I didn't know they still had their heads on. No big deal, just peel them off." Of course, if was no big deal to him; he did not have to help since he was going to be busy getting married soon.

We made a makeshift aisle, got married in our hotel suite, and then had a party. At the same time as our reception and rainstorm in Key West, the north was getting pounded with a blizzard. Little did we realize that everyone was going to get stuck with us the very next day.

The party went on until late into the evening, and everyone came back to our room for breakfast the next morning. During our morning meal, we discovered the intensity of the storm and learned that all airplanes were grounded and roads for miles around were closed.

"Oh, my God! How is everyone going to get back for Valentine's weekend?" asked Cliff during breakfast.

"We aren't," was the unanimous reply.

"But we need to get our clubs opened for the weekend, and all the important people are here," he said.

In all of the chaos and speculation, we decided to rent a car for our club manager and head doorman so they could drive to Miami and try to get on the next plane north, whenever that would be.

My parents and my brother, along with his wife, had already arranged to spend an extra night at the hotel so they were not really affected. The others stuck in Key West had to check out of their rooms because the hotel was booked completely. Everyone was also short on funds (this was long before ATMs were everywhere), and we had to help them out so they could fly home. Four people moved into our suite, making the honeymoon quite a memory!

After we dined that evening, all the girls and gay men went shopping in my closet for an impromptu fashion show. Someone stepped up and took over as emcee, hosting the show. Some people had on my dresses, and others had on my lingerie. We feasted on the laughter—something we all needed to do.

"No one will ever top this honeymoon," was all I could say as I sipped champagne in my negligee, laughing. "The snowstorm made this wedding that much more fun!"

As the night ended and everyone was tucked into their place on the couch or floor, Cliff and I lay in bed and just laughed. "Will anyone ever believe this?" I asked him.

"No, of course, no one will believe you," he said before we fell asleep.

The next morning, we awoke to singing. "I think it is coming from the bathroom," I told Cliff as we roused from a deep slumber. "I will go take a peek." I knocked on the bathroom door, and for a moment the singing stopped.

"Come on in," said Donald, Cliff's best man.

I opened the door and found Donald with a big bubble bath around him, candles lit all over the room, and a cigarette hanging out of his mouth. All I could do was laugh and yell out to everyone else in our honeymoon suite, "Come see this!"

Donald did not miss a beat. "Morning to us all," he said and then kept on singing, bathing, and smoking. We shut the door, and I shook my head. My honeymoon was getting funnier by the hour.

After another night, we were able to get everyone on a plane and then head back up north by car to continue with our crazy lives. I stashed this memory, but not too deeply—I wanted to keep it for a frequent reference and a smile!

CHAPTER 33

ROCK SHRIMP STORY...

Before we headed back to New Jersey, we dined at a little spot that served a dish of "rock shrimp," something we had never tried before.

Cliff and I loved to vacation in Key West. We enjoyed trips there at least once yearly since early in our relationship, usually driving since Cliff did not care to fly. For some reason, though, we decided to fly down there once after we had been married a few years.

I had not had any medical problems for about five years, and my life seemed normal. After spending so much time being sick though, the signs, symptoms and pain of the past always lingered in the back of my mind. Finally, I felt able to give regular life a chance. I was enjoying being healthy, happily married and involved in everything my husband did. With two nightclubs running full time under the watchful eye of managers and staff we trusted, we were able to take an extra long vacation.

The weather was picture perfect in Key West, and our decision to enjoy those extra days by not driving down was a good one. Before we headed back to New Jersey, we dined at a little spot that served a dish of "rock shrimp," something we had never tried before. The shell of this shrimp was as hard as a stone crab and difficult to crack in order to get the shrimp out. I struggled with the cracking but enjoyed the shrimp just the same. During the flight home that night, I started to feel funny but shrugged it off, thinking I was worried that Cliff was not okay with flying. Feeling woozy, I walked to the rest room and discovered that I was passing blood. I was shocked. I couldn't figure out what could possibly be causing the bleeding but told myself I would be fine by the time we got home.

"I must be bleeding internally," I said when I returned to Cliff at our seats. "When I inserted my catheter to relieve myself, I only saw blood come through. It seemed like a large amount of blood, but I don't feel ill or weak. I have no idea how this could have happened, but let's see how I feel by the time we land."

I tried to relax in my seat and not get too upset. We had about an hour left in our flight, so we were not too far away at this point.

"We have to get to the hospital right away," he told me.

"I am not going to the hospital after such a nice vacation. I will be fine," I told him stubbornly, and that was the end of the conversation. We hardly spoke a word for the rest of the flight.

I continued to pass blood through the night and was feeling much worse by morning. I finally consented, and we headed to The Children's Hospital of Philadelphia first thing in the morning.

I felt I wanted to be in a familiar place with my doctors even though I was an adult. "They will steer me in the right direction," I told Cliff. When we arrived, they agreed to treat me as a patient since I had been there for so many years.

After checking in, we found out my surgeon was away until Monday and that another doctor was thinking about opening me up to take a look at the damage—an exploratory kind of thing. I refused to be treated by anyone other than Dr. Templeton and told the resident on duty that I would wait for him. So for the next three days, I shared a room with an infant in a crib—how weird to be a patient in a children's hospital when I was married and in my 20s! I spent most of my time helping the kids do crafts and drawings.

Cliff visited me every day, and the nurses remarked about my beautiful tan. "That's what two weeks in the Keys will bring you," I kept telling them. I felt better after three days, and the bleeding seemed to have subsided, but I was still concerned about what may have been going on inside of me.

Dr. Templeton stepped into my room on Monday morning, surprised to see me. It had been at least three years since I had been in for care.

"I looked at the tests that were taken when you arrived at the hospital and read the reports the other doctors wrote up. Since you are feeling better and the bleeding is subsiding, it was probably something you ate. You mentioned eating rock shrimp on your vacation and you must have swallowed a small piece of shell, which cut you somewhere when you swallowed it," he continued. "Your insides are apparently healing themselves, so we will send you home. If you feel sick again, though, come right back in."

As we were gathering up my belongings, I told Cliff that I felt I wasted a weekend in the hospital.

"It was just a couple days and better to be safe than sorry," He replied. We went home with no more problems from that day on, figuring I must have been cut from a shell. I made a mental note to be more careful in the future.

CHAPTER 34

TIME TO MOVE ON

❦

Cliff and I spoke periodically about moving to a warmer climate.

Cliff and I spoke periodically about moving to a warmer climate. We worked hard in our business and decided that someday we would sell what we had, pack up, and maybe open up a business in Florida. This conversation happened often especially when things were stressful. We did not share our plans for the future with anyone other than immediate family so that we would not upset our customers and loyal staff members. Over the years, we watched Atlantic City's slow growth, thinking that eventually a casino would buy our street and we would be able to fulfill our dreams. Cliff would often say, "When the time is right and the deal is right, we'll know it."

About 6–7 years later, we finally got an offer that was worthy of serious consideration. The offer for both nightclubs was our dream, and we knew that this was the time when our investments and hard work were going to finally pay off. Negotiations began, and after a few months, an agreement was reached.

We had a month to close and completely strip the clubs down to a shell, which meant we could sell all of the contents separately. The other business owners on the street who sold did just that, but we were the only ones who negotiated to leave the contents intact until after settlement.

"What if something happens and we get the buildings back?" was all Cliff could think about. "I don't want to disturb anything until after settlement, when we have the check in our hand. Then we will go in and tear out the contents." Our lawyer agreed, and in the agreement of sale, we were protected for 30 days after settlement.

We knew we had to throw a huge "goodbye" party. At Cliff's suggestion, we decided on back-to-back parties on different nights in one weekend so that we could say goodbye to our customers.

Everyone who had ever come to either place wanted to be with us on those nights. We were extremely crowded, and the night flew by without many problems. The main issue was having the entire staff on guard because people seemed to feel they needed souvenirs from the walls and/or a piece of furniture.

"Watching people for theft is harder than I ever thought," I told Cliff at the end of two days of parties, each party about eight hours long.

It was mentally exhausting to bid goodbye, but we headed off to an extended vacation to await settlement. We made the road trip to Key West for a two-week rest, which was well deserved and earned. After the first three or four days, Cliff did not feel very well but thought he had just gotten too much sun. We both walked back into our hotel room and Cliff headed for the bed.

"I think I need to lay down for a while." He headed for a quick shower and then closed the drapes to darken the room and take a nap. While he was napping, I took a shower and laid down to read for a while. About two hours later he woke up and rolled over toward me. It must have been about 5:00 p.m., and he looked like his face was on fire. "Please, take me to the hospital. I need a doctor," Cliff said when he looked at me.

"Okay, are you sure?" I asked.

"Yes, we need to go now!"

We raced off to the small hospital that looked like a little office building but seemed very well equipped. Cliff was burning up with fever and we were taken in almost immediately.

"Your husband has such a high fever, and we need to get to the bottom of it," said the attending physician.

I was puzzled, thinking he had flu-like systems, but the staff seemed to think otherwise. They began to check him for lesions and sores, which again puzzled both of us. They asked about foreign travel and then, after some x-rays, came the really uncomfortable questions. "Did you ever have relations with a male at any time?" the doctor asked bluntly. I almost fell off my chair. I had no idea where this was going but sat quietly while Cliff answered. Of course, his answer was "no," but none of this was clicking for either of us. The year was 1986, and after the doctors found out we owned a gay nightclub, they assumed they had a case of a new disease on their hands.

Every doctor that entered the emergency room seemed puzzled and kept asking the same questions. Cliff showed all the signs of this new disease, and they interrogated him because of his symptoms. As a married couple, the personal sexual questions were very uncomfortable to answer. Cliff had pneumonia a few times during his life, and his most recent bout was about a month prior to our vacation. He is asthmatic, too, so he is monitored on a regular basis.

Cliff was admitted to the hospital, and put on a strong mix of drugs to reduce the fever and antibiotics to fight whatever was making him ill. Days passed, and he was hallucinating and burning up. I decided to call his doctors at home to share what was going on with them and get some advice. Cliff was too sick to move, and his doctors up north told me that the treatment he was receiving was fine. Rest and a strong mix of antibiotics were important, and it seemed that he was in good hands.

After about a week of the same treatments, Cliff told me, "No matter what, we need to go to settlement on the clubs so we do not jeopardize our future." We arranged for our lawyer to send me papers for power of attorney so that I could fly home for settlement while Cliff recovered. Without fax machines and computers, it took extra time. But I left Key West with the promise to Cliff that I would return without the two nightclubs.

My whirlwind three-day trip ended with the other party forfeiting their deposits to us and not coming to settlement. I was able to pay off a mortgage on one of the clubs, keep Cliff's partner Donna happy with a check, and go back to Key West to find Cliff in our hotel waiting for me. They determined he had very bad pneumonia, but that he should get tested for this new disease upon our return home because of our "contact" with the gay community. We did not believe that Cliff was infected but did not take any chances since the doctors at that time were uncertain as to what this "new" disease was.

After a few days building up strength for the long trip home, we drove back to New Jersey, and the first thing we did was have Cliff tested. The lung specialist appointment that followed was reassuring because he said it was, "wise to get tested, but you could not have recovered in ten days like you did if you were positive." When the results trickled in a few weeks later, the doctor was correct: Cliff did not have this new horrific disease.

As much as we were relieved, we began to notice that more and more people we knew or who worked for us were extremely ill, and many were dying quickly. One funeral after another—mostly for gay men—began to work on us emotionally. The pattern became more noticeable, and we all began to wonder what terrible thing could they be passing to one another and how?

"How could the world ignore what is happening?" I asked Cliff one day. *Why is it only gay people? How could this be happening to just one kind of person?*

Little by little, business began to slip. We could not understand what we were doing wrong, and then slowly, the realization hit. People thought that only gay people were dying from this new disease. "We cannot go to a gay club," I heard repeatedly.

It may be from touching, kissing, or sharing, was what most people thought. Time and again, people made comments to me about things like drinking from a straw and not putting my lips to the glasses in the gay night club.

I wondered how a deadly disease could be spread so simply. If that was the case, we would all be dead, right? Cliff and I worked side by side with gay and straight people every day—and had for years. "You really do not know who you come into contact with on a daily basis," I would say, but no one would listen. Our gay friends were scared to come to the club for fear of catching something, and our straight friends would not come for the same reason. Slowly, business dropped and we began to struggle. After not going to settlement, we had been forced to reopen and were stuck.

One evening while eating dinner and watching the news, Cliff and I learned that the new disease that was killing gay men now had a name. They tracked it as best as they could to try and find the origin of the virus, something they were still working on, but it finally had a name: HIV and AIDS. We were soon to learn the difference between the two, and why gay men were the ones who were suffering. What we did not know at that point was that not long after the discovery, the virus was going to infect women, IV drug users, and children.

With the amount of gay friends and employees we had, we both knew how very serious HIV and AIDS were. Donald, the best man at our wedding who I found singing in our bathtub the night after our wedding, contracted HIV and developed AIDS. On a visit to see him right before he passed away, I thought I was going to lose it. Cliff and I knew when we entered his home that this would be the last time we would see Donald, and we needed to say goodbye. Although I had been to many funerals of friends who had passed away from AIDS, I had not seen them right before death. AIDS attacks the entire body and eats away at everything, leaving you emaciated. By the time we finished our visit and headed home, I was very ill. Cliff had to pull the car over during our three-hour ride home so I could vomit. It was devastating for me to see Donald that way. He was a kid when he began working for Cliff sweeping floors and ended up being a manager of our gay club. Donald had been very healthy, but he was also promiscuous. By the time we all learned what AIDS was, he had already contracted the disease. He was just 35 when he died.

We eventually shut the gay club down and rented it out for other kinds of parties. Thankfully, we were still able to make a decent living out of the Chez for a few years until I got pregnant and Cliff had another chance to sell it.

CHAPTER 35

LET'S HAVE A BABY

For the first time in my life, it seemed that a decision I had planned my life around had been turned upside down.

When I was a child, my parents questioned Dr. Koop about my odds of getting pregnant.

"Alesia should have no problem becoming pregnant. All of her organs are intact and she should be able to conceive and live a very normal life," Dr. Koop told both Mom and Dad one day before my surgery. Neither of my parents ever questioned him or anyone else again after that.

Seven years went by in our marriage, and it seemed that I was not going to experience pregnancy. About five years into our marriage, I had voiced some of my own questions. "Cliff, I struggle with thoughts of wanting and not wanting a child, so I think I will see a specialist to find out if it is possible, and then we can take it from there."

Cliff was supportive of my wanting to have a child, but did not seem too upset if we did not. "We work all night and sleep all day, we are not home for long periods of time, and I tend to feel it may not be in our best interest to have a child at this time," he stated one day while we were discussing it. "If you really would like a child, I am supportive of that even though I already have a daughter. If it is not possible, we still have her."

I made a few appointments with a specialist in Philadelphia and went to find more answers. During my first appointment, I answered many personal questions about our lives.

"How often do you have a period? How often do you have intercourse?"

Of course, I expected some questions but was uncomfortable answering them because I was young and not prepared for such candor. After a few tests, the doctors could not determine anything wrong and told me that I could continue to investigate further if that was what we wanted to do.

On my drive home, I realized the doctor was implying artificial insemination. I felt uneasy about "artificial" anything and still was not certain how Cliff felt about becoming a father again. Before I reached home, I decided that if God wanted me to have a child, he would bless me naturally. If not, then I was not meant to be a mother.

About a month or so later I woke up with an uneasy feeling. "My breasts are so swollen, and I feel crappy even though my period just ended two weeks ago," I told Cliff that morning. "I can't figure out if I am coming down with a cold or not..."

Cliff watched me walk across the room. "You're probably pregnant," he said with a laugh.

"Yeah, right," was all I could say, but then I looked straight at him and asked, "Could it be? I finally kind of bagged the pregnancy thing and now I get pregnant?"

Later, we returned from the drug store with two pregnancy tests. I marched into the bathroom and came out holding the stick, waiting for what seemed like forever. "Positive...that is impossible!" I yelled at him as I headed back into the bathroom to do the second test.

"I told you you're pregnant. And look, the box says 99.9 % accurate," he yelled through the door.

"Okay, this one is positive, too. Now what?!" I asked in a strained and shaky voice. "I better call the doctor for blood work."

I went to spend the night with my parents before heading to Phila to the doctor. When I called the doctor's office the next morning, the nurse told me, "The store tests are very, very accurate, but if it makes you feel better, come on in." After the blood test, I headed back to my parents' house to await my results. For some reason, I was in complete denial. It may have something to do with the fact that I had always been a planner. When I decided I was not going to wear the regular external iliostomy bag, I found the Kock pouch and set my mind on it. It was the same when I decided I was not going to be able to get pregnant. I truly believed that God had made that decision for me. For the first time in my life, it seemed that a decision I had planned my life around had been turned upside down.

The next morning, the phone rang. I picked it up—only to be congratulated by the nurse, confirming my pregnancy. "I am not sure if you should congratulate me or not." I quickly recovered and understood that yes, we were having a baby.

Cliff was so excited that he was gushing over the phone when I called him. When I got home that evening, he was still bubbling over with excitement, and I began to relax about what was going to be a new turn in our lives.

My pregnancy was uneventful for the first four and a half months. My medical team had never had a pregnant patient with my surgical history, so we set out to find someone with similar issues who had carried and delivered a baby. One of the nurses who worked for my gynecologist found someone who had the identical surgeries as I had, then carried to full term and delivered. We spoke a few times, comparing our surgeries and other similarities between us. My doctors and I breathed a bit easier; we all felt ready to move ahead and stop worrying.

"Alesia, let's move on." my doctor told me. "Rest easy and take this pregnancy one day at a time. This young lady had a wonderful experience, so we have that to look forward to."

I stopped working nights after the first few months because I could not stay awake past 9:00 in the evening. By the time I napped, got up at midnight and showered, and drove to work, I was almost asleep in the office. It was easier for Cliff to leave me home, which was better for my health anyway.

One night at about 4–5 months into the pregnancy, I woke about 3:00 a.m. with horrible pains in my back and stomach. I tossed and turned, afraid to awake Cliff. After about two hours of unbearable pain, which seemed to be getting worse, I woke him and half-hysterically told him, "The pain is so bad!" I gasped between breaths and started crying. "I am unsure if we are having a baby and I am in labor, or if I am having a miscarriage!"

Not sure about what to do, he got the phone book and called our gynecologist. He put me on the phone, and the doctor asked me if I wanted to go to a local hospital or come to Philadelphia. My feeling at that point was

I suffered for two hours already; I could make the ride to Philly, and whatever was happening, I would be with doctors I knew and trusted.

The hour and fifteen minute ride to the hospital took 30 minutes. We intentionally drove fast, figuring that we would get pulled over and then escorted to the hospital. I was scared and ill and all I could tell Cliff was, "Get me there!" We went through every red light, on the medians, around cars, and never once got pulled over. I vomited all the way; thank God we thought to bring plastic bags.

I was taken in through the emergency entrance, but went directly to the delivery floor. The nurses hooked me up to baby monitors within minutes of my arrival. I was contracting but the doctors immediately began shots to control the labor since I was only 4 ½ months pregnant. I could not stop vomiting, and the staff finally inserted a tube into my nose, down my throat, and into my stomach, which made me feel better. That—along with some mild pain medication—allowed me to rest comfortably so the delivery room nurses could take x-rays.

After hours of waiting, my gynecologist came in and told me I had a bowel obstruction, probably from scar tissue from past surgeries. Because my organs were beginning to move to make room for the baby, my intestinal tract became trapped and twisted. In my case, the only way out for the bile and juices created in my intestines was through vomit.

"So what do we do now?" I asked. Cliff was sitting quietly on the sidelines, probably too scared to say anything at all.

"Well, I thought it would be best to leave you be, wait a bit and see if the obstruction can fix itself while you rest," the doctor said.

"Sounds good, but how long?" I asked.

"I am not sure, so we will play it by ear and keep an eye on you," he answered.

After three days of agony and fear, a new team of three surgeons—Dr. Horowitz, Dr. Rosenberg, and Dr. Goldberg—came in to introduce themselves and speak to Cliff and me. They specialized in intestinal problems and even though I was pregnant, they had to do something about the obstruction. They explained that there was no change in my condition and that surgery was the only answer.

"How can you do that while I am pregnant?" I asked. I felt uncertain and just plain scared.

Dr. Horowitz summed it up. "We will do the best we can, but we have to do something. You will get worse if we don't do anything. We have spoken to other doctors about your case, and we all agree that this is the only answer."

I immediately began to let my thoughts get the best of me. I decided not to share my turmoil with anyone, including my husband. *What if they ask us to choose between losing me or the baby? What if they tell me that there is something horribly wrong with the baby, what will we do?* Cliff was wrapped up in his own thoughts, possibly the same as mine, but remained quiet as the evening wore on. He left eventually, only to return bright and early before surgery. I was unable to sleep the entire night worrying about our future.

The next morning, as they wheeled me to surgery, Cliff wished me luck and gave me a soft kiss.

By the time I was wheeled into the operating room, I was trembling, but I was back in my room before I knew it. I was hooked up to so many machines and monitors that I began to wonder what had happened to me.

"Why am I in a birthing room?" I asked the nurse when I awoke, trying to focus on my surroundings.

"We are keeping an eye on your contractions, and I will be here for the next 24–48 hours to make sure you do not move. If you need anything, I can get it for you immediately," she told me. After awhile, she bathed me, brushed my hair, and managed to make me comfortable. It was the middle of the night.

In the morning, the doctors came by and Dr. Horowitz explained how well the surgery had gone.

"We lifted her out and placed her on your side, cleaned up the obstruction and placed her back inside your belly," he explained

I got excited and asked, "It's a girl?"

"No, no," he said. "We could not see through the sack carrying your baby. I just want you to have a girl. You see, my wife and I just had a baby girl, and she is so very sweet. I wish the same experience for you. Now, all we do is wait. You need to stay still for as long as you can to avoid labor, and we will try to get you home," he told me.

One of my fondest memories of my mother came during this time. Mom came to the hospital every day with my father. My dad would stay for a while, but Mom would spend the entire day either hanging out with me or helping care for me. She was not in the best of health, but she sat from morning until night, keeping me company. We talked, sat quietly, and filled our time just being together.

It was a rough two weeks, during which I was restricted to bed so that my body could heal and my baby would stay safe inside me for as long as possible.

I began to refer to myself as a "professional patient" who knew the "drill" of being in bed for long periods of time. I thought back to the weeks I spent not being allowed out of bed until I ate something and remembered what time to expect the doctors in the morning, how long it took to have medications brought to the floor, how long x-rays usually took, and how long we waited for results. Although I was in a different hospital now, it all came back to me instantly as if it was yesterday. Falling into my old routine, I bathed, ate, and walked. It was kind of eerie to go through it and be okay about everything happening. I even felt at ease when they came to give me news, good or bad. It was as if I was in a time warp and came up with that "professional patient" label to try to bring some humor to my days.

My body was frail but I was ready to go home and finish carrying this baby and try to get back to normal. I was told to eat as many meals a day as I could because I had lost so much weight, but the baby's heartbeat remained normal through this entire ordeal. Also, I was told to do nothing more than just a little walking. My surgical team said that I would not be able to carry full term because of what I had been through, but the secret was to keep the baby inside of me for as long a possible.

I went home and did as I was told; ate all I could, took short walks, and watched as many movies as I could stand, including all the Marilyn Monroe movies we had in the house.

During the rest of my pregnancy, I had a few trips to the emergency room but was always sent back home. By the time a woman is nine months pregnant, looking down past the top of her belly is impossible. I could not see or maneuver the catheter into the area needed to insert it. The pouch that had been built inside of me was lying on my uterus. Because of this, when the baby began to grow and my organs moved to make room for the baby's growth, the pouch became crushed against the uterus, therefore not allowing the catheter to slide into place and backing up my digestive track. The doctors got things working and kept me from having to deliver the baby too early, which also gave me more time to regain my strength after the surgery.

Since I wanted to deliver with my doctors in Philadelphia, they suggested that I spend my ninth month close to the hospital—just in case. It worked out well because I got to spend some quality time with my parents, and Cliff came up every few days to be with me when he could get away. Everything seemed to be going nicely other than the discomfort of being in my ninth month of pregnancy. Then the phone rang.

"Hi, Alesia." Cliff's voice seemed shaken.

"Is everything all right?" I asked.

"Well, I was leaving the club this afternoon on my way to the bank when I was approached by a guy with an ice pick or knife or something, and he wanted my briefcase," he said, his voice cracking.

I hesitated but asked, "Then what happened?"

"My reaction was not to give in. I wouldn't let go of the briefcase, so he stabbed me with whatever he was holding, pushed me down, and took off."

"Are you all right?" I couldn't believe what I was hearing. What else could happen to us? Tears were forming in my eyes.

"A cop came by, saw me on the ground, asked me what the guy looked like, and took off while I was lying there. I got in the car and headed for the Atlantic City Hospital. They handed me a paper towel for the blood, told me to sit down, and left me in the waiting room," he told me. He hesitated before continuing. "I waited about an hour, got in the car, and came home."

"Are you crazy? You need to get that looked at right away!" I was almost screaming.

"Maybe tomorrow," he replied casually.

"No! You need to go now!" I was frantic.

After I hung up, I called our neighbor, Glenn, and had him go take Cliff to the hospital. They had to re-open the stab wound, clean it out, and check for punctures. It was close to his lungs, but there were no punctures, thank

God. All I could think of was that we were going to have a baby in a few days and he decided to do something foolish and not get a stab wound taken care of immediately. It upset me that I was not home and that all I could do was be supportive over the phone. He continued to heal nicely, and I continued to grow our baby.

To further complicate things, my father-in-law, who had been in a nursing home for a few years with Alzheimer's, began to fail. A week after Cliff was stabbed, his father passed away. It was sad that he would not get a chance to see his only grandson. Even though he did not approve of our relationship in the beginning, he ended up liking me and getting along with me very well before his mind began to slip away. Because I was up in Philadelphia, I insisted on making the hour-long trip to attend his funeral.

It's funny how "old wives' tales" travel from generation to generation. All of my mother's Jewish friends told her I should not attend the funeral so late in my pregnancy.

"How can I not attend my own father-in-law's funeral?" I asked them while they sat around my parents' house drinking coffee.

"It's bad luck," one of them said. "Especially if you walk on the graves in your ninth month."

"And do not look directly at his grave, or the baby will be born with strawberry birthmarks on its face," another added seriously.

"With all due respect, are you all crazy? How could you all look at me and tell me this bullshit, only upsetting me more before I go to his funeral? I don't care what any of you think. I am going, whether you think I should or not!" And that was that.

At his funeral the following day, not only did I walk across all the graves I could, I also looked directly at his grave during the short service and then walked across all the graves I could step on while walking back to the car. When we pulled away from the cemetery, I had a big smile on my face.

When I gave birth the following week, my baby was beautiful. I not only made it *to* my due date, I almost went past it and had to be induced. The doctors wanted to avoid a Cesarean Section—another surgery—so I was again hooked up to IVs, this time with medication to bring on contractions.

My parents had taken me to the hospital the night before, and Cliff came up the following morning. By the end of that day, despite six hours of pushing, I ended up with a C-section. Though I never admitted it to him, I was afraid Cliff might pass out in the delivery room. My good friend, Terry, spent about 10 hours with us but left before they decided to do the surgery, so Cliff ended up not only pulling for me but also telling me it was the most exciting day of his life.

When Johnathan came out at 8 pounds and 4 ounces, he looked so round I called him "my little turkey." The same surgeon who did my bowel obstruction surgery just four months before was called in, too, in case of complications. Thankfully, his services weren't necessary. He told me it was exciting to see our son delivered, and he came to visit us again a few days after birth.

Naming our baby was an exciting and difficult job. In my religion, Judaism, we normally name a child after someone who has passed, out of respect for the dead. In Cliff's religion, Protestant, people normally name a child after someone in the family who is alive. We compromised by choosing Johnathan after Cliff's dad John, which is actually also Cliff's first name. We then took the first letter from my grandmother's name, Nancy, and came up with Nevil for a middle name.

Because of my medical history, the doctors decided that cutting me in the customary C-section way wasn't a good idea. A typical C-section incision runs horizontally on the lower abdomen. I, however, ended up with another scar just a hairline away from my other scars, running from belly button to my groin. Every other surgery I have had, the doctors were considerate enough to keep cutting next to the old scar. As a result, I appear to have had only one surgery instead of a railroad track across my belly. At 29 years old, this surgery was the easiest—and I had beautiful baby to show for it!

CHAPTER 36

NOT ANOTHER SURGERY

Kessler Memorial Hospital was about twelve minutes from our home. It took about two hours to register and get the X-rays and results.

After Johnathan was born, the first two years were like any other for a first time mother. I changed diapers, stopped the crying, and slept very little. This was something that all women experience to get to the good part...a beautiful, perfect baby that you cannot stop staring at because you brought this wonderful creature into the world. I am still amazed that I carried this human being inside of me. I cried when I first looked at him because I could not really believe that my husband and I really did this.

It was a cold winter night. I was feeling a bit funny but could not put my finger on what was wrong. Johnathan was about two years old and getting ready for bed. After trying to sell the Chez for two years, Cliff learned that the Alcoholic Beverage Control Board was going to deny the potential buyers a liquor license, which meant they wouldn't buy the club. In the state of New Jersey, when you want to sell your liquor license, there is an investigation into all parties who are involved. Apparently, one of the guys named on the license was found to have some kind of mob ties. Our hopes of moving—possibly to Florida—and trying to live more of a normal life now suddenly seemed far away. Cliff thought I was not feeling well that night because of the stress over the news he had just given me.

"My stomach hurts; it must be something I ate," I told him as I put Johnathan in his room. "I am going to lie on the couch for a while to see if it passes."

"You'll be fine. We'll be fine," Cliff said. "It will all work out—promise. Stop worrying."

After awhile, I felt as if I was in labor. The pain was getting more and more intense, while I was worrying about being considerate of Cliff.

"Are you okay," he asked? "Do you think we should call the doctor or go to the emergency room? What kind of pain is it? I can see it is really bad by your facial expressions."

I waited until about 11:00 that night before I finally gave in. "Cliff, let's get to the hospital. The pain is really bad. It's the same pain I had when I was pregnant with Johnathan and had the obstruction. Cliff, I am so scared, I don't know if I can go through this again."

"Let's not jump the gun just yet," he said. He quickly called our neighbor and friend Terry to come over and stay with Johnathan while we went to the hospital. He then called the doctors in Philadelphia, who told us to get x-rays immediately at our nearest hospital.

Kessler Memorial Hospital was about twelve minutes from our home. It took about two hours to register and get the X-rays and results. I was not even able to stand straight for the pictures because the pain was getting more intense, so the nurse finally offered me a shot for pain. As we waited for the doctor to return, I curled up on the gurney. "Cliff, I cannot do this, I cannot go through this." All he could do was watch me suffer.

A few minutes after the shot began to relieve the pain, the doctor came in and told us, "You have a bowel obstruction, and we have spoken to your doctors in Philadelphia. They will have a bed waiting for you either now or first thing in the morning. It depends on the level of pain, but you need to get up there soon."

"I think the pain is gone and I will be fine," I told them. "I think we can go home."

"Not feeling the pain is a mask from the medication," said the doctor. "You will have a bed whenever you arrive."

"Let's go home and get some sleep," I told Cliff. "May as well wait until morning since I feel so good, right?"

"Are you sure?" he asked. "Terry is already babysitting…we are on the road…it is up to you."

Cliff must have figured it made more sense to keep going than to drive all the way back home when it was inevitable that we were going to have to leave again to head up to Philadelphia, which was a bit over an hour from our home.

Still, I persisted. "Let's go home, sleep a little and head to Philadelphia in the morning. I am fine."

As we were driving home from the hospital at about 2:00 a.m., I was in complete denial that I was really sick again. When we arrived home, Terry was asleep on our couch and left after we assured her that we were okay.

About a half hour later, Cliff and I crawled into bed and tried to get some sleep. By then, the shot they gave me for pain was beginning to wear off and I was soon in agony again. Cliff felt me moving around and heard my shallow breathing.

"Are you okay?" he asked. He already knew the answer but asked anyway.

"No," I moaned. "I am so sorry about this. I really thought I was okay and that we could at least get some sleep before going to Philadelphia."

"Call your parents," he said. "We'll drop Johnathan off at their house and head up to the hospital." As I reached for the phone to call my mother, another sharp pain hit me and I felt as if I was going to pass out.

"Mom, I am so sorry to wake you, but I have to get to the hospital. I have another obstruction, and I am in terrible pain. We are leaving in about five minutes and need to drop Johnathan off at your house."

"Okay," she said. "Just take it slow and be careful driving. Is there anything else we can do?"

"No, just be there. Thanks," I managed before I hung up to wait for Cliff.

I grabbed my medical supplies and my pillow—all I could think about needing—and some bags in case I got sick in the car. Downstairs in Johnathan's bedroom, I gathered diapers, a change of clothes, and some juice in case he woke up.

Cliff drove as fast as possible, reassuring me that it was okay that we had gone home first. I was crying and short of breath from the pain. Johnathan slept the entire way, and I held a bag just below my face since I knew I was going to be sick.

"Are you okay?" Cliff asked seeing me holding up the bag.

"Just get there!" was all I managed to say.

By the time we got to Philly, I was vomiting and told Cliff to skip my parents' house and drop me off at the hospital first. "I can't wait any longer," I told him. He dropped me off at the emergency room and left with Johnathan.

Right away, the doctors got me onto a gurney and told me they would try to make me comfortable. I knew the NG tube was coming next, but I was actually looking forward to it because it would give me relief. I knew it was all they could do until they surgically fixed the obstruction.

"Hold still, keep swallowing and try to relax."

I squeezed the nurses' hands on either side of me and kept my eyes closed. All of the sudden, the tube was sent up my nose, down my throat and I was projectile vomiting all over the place...and then it was over.

"I feel a bit better already," I told them as they tried to clean me up. I looked up and saw Cliff waiting in the doorway. I wondered what he was thinking at that moment. Between me, our baby, and a business to worry about, he looked tired.

The nurses and doctors left while we waited for a room. I began to doze, and Cliff waited by my bed to speak to my doctors when they arrived later.

"Why not go over to my parents for a nap?" I asked him.

"I'll wait until the doctors come, and then I'll leave and come back later tonight," he told me.

Not long afterward, we were in my room, and I was sedated. In the haze, I heard someone ask, "What the hell are you doing here again?" I looked up to see Dr. Horowitz and Dr. Rosenberg, two of the surgeons who had seen me through the surgery during my pregnancy. Dr. Horowitz had a wonderful bedside manner, whereas Dr. Rosenberg was all business. "Again, scar tissue, now this time from your delivery..." he explained. "You'll need surgery to clear your blocked intestines. We will schedule it for tomorrow and—with no complications—get you out of here in about a week."

I was so tired—and happy to be almost pain free, and Cliff was relieved to be able to leave and come back in the morning. He had to take care of our pets, check on Johnathan, and give my parents the news. He drove the hour home while I waited until morning for surgery.

On the way to surgery the following day, I was not thinking about anything but getting home and never having to endure this again. The next thing I knew, Cliff was by my side, telling me, "You'll feel better in a few days."

I was a bit drowsy, but Cliff and I waited to hear what the doctors were going to say when Dr. Horowitz came in during rounds the next morning. "The surgery was quick and easy," he told us. "We saw a small piece of scar tissue wrapped around your intestine."

"Can you explain why this happened again?" I asked.

"It seems like a fluke that it happened, but we will keep an eye on you for the next week. You should be able to go home and recover without any problems," he explained. That was good enough for me.

Cliff came to visit every day, and so did my parents. A couple of times, they even brought Johnathan to say hello. All of my friends and family visited, as well, and it did not take more than a few days for me to begin to feel better. My parents took turns visiting without Johnathan every day, and Cliff came late in the day after most everyone else left.

During one of his visits, Cliff brought up the inevitable. "I had to go back to the club and tell the guys I am going to take back over the business," my husband told me. "We're trying to work out a deal so that we are partners. Although I own the building, we can still have a legal partnership. That way I will not have to work as much, and you can worry about getting better and taking care of Johnathan. The problem now is that the guys trying to buy the business made such a mess of the bills, it will take forever for me to straighten it all out. I will become the organizer, working during the day and not working nights unless I want to. That makes it a winning situation for all of us. They can still operate it, and we will be partners in the split."

"That works for me if that's the only choice we have," I told him. "We have to make the best of the situation."

"Like I always say," he continued, "operating a successful business is better than shutting it down and waiting for it to sell." I had to agree. We needed to keep the money coming in.

Cliff got busy with the business again, and I began to feel well enough to eat. Ten days after surgery, my doctors told me that they thought I could go home that day if I wanted to. Surprisingly, I didn't leap at the opportunity. I felt a bit funny—flu-like or something—but thought it could be anxiety about leaving.

"Maybe I've picked up something here in the hospital," I mentioned to my nurse after the doctors had left. Still, like always, I told myself I would be fine. I called Cliff right away.

"Bring me clothes," I told him as he picked up the phone. "I am coming home today."

"I am headed to Atlantic City to the club first thing, and then I will be there to get you," he said. "It is supposed to snow really bad today, so I will bring you some boots. They are calling for about 12 inches."

"Hurry up so I do not get snowed in," I laughed. "See ya later. I love you."

As the day slowly went by, I began to feel ill. I thought to myself that I was, indeed, getting sick with a cold or flu, but I wanted to be home so badly I decided not to say anything. By lunchtime, I had a slight fever and felt nauseous. The nurses began to notice and asked why I hadn't eaten anything.

"I don't feel well," I confessed to one of them as I looked out the window, watching the heavy snow and wondering if Cliff would be able to make it.

"Try to eat something, and you will feel better," she said. "We will check your temperature in a little while."

I headed across the room to my bed where the tray of food awaited me. Although I was not hungry, I began to eat, figuring she might be right. About halfway through the meal, she came back to check on me. I remember looking up at her and feeling a bit "green." Within a minute of her approaching me, I vomited all over the bed, the tray, and myself. It happened so quickly that I did not have a chance to prepare myself and was as surprised as she was when it happened. I had to lie back in the bed as she helped clean me up. She felt my head; I was beginning to sweat.

"You are not going anywhere today," she told me. "I am calling your doctors right away."

Barely able to speak, I agreed. I was a mess from being sick and needed to lie down before I got sick again. When I looked out the window now, the snow was falling fast and heavy and the wind was already creating drifts that I could see from the 5th floor. Indeed, I wasn't leaving the hospital. Instead,

134

I was taken down for x-rays again. By mid-afternoon, I was back in bed with a fever and unable to eat.

I must have dozed off for a while and when I looked up, Dr. Horowitz was standing beside my bed. "Alesia, I have some bad news," he said. "The x-rays show another obstruction, so we have you scheduled for surgery tonight. We foresee no problems, so we can assume that we this will take care of it. We'll send you home as soon as possible."

"Surgery? What are you talking about?"

"Another band of scar tissue must have wrapped itself around you again. The last surgery was about 45 minutes, which leads me to believe that this one should be about the same, okay?"

"If I have no choice, I guess it's okay. But I need to get in touch with my husband. He thinks he is coming here to take me home," I told the doctor. "Let me call and track him down."

I began with calling my mother—so upset that I had a hard time talking about it. She promised to take care of Johnathan while I was in the hospital to make it easier for Cliff, but I also knew that she was not very well. My father assured me that he would help and that I should not worry about anything but myself. As I hung up the phone, I tried to figure out how to reach Cliff.

I called our home. There was no answer, but I left a message. Next, I called the club in Atlantic City. Cliff had been there but left, mentioning he would stop at home to let the dogs out then head to the hospital to pick me up and take me home.

Since the weather was so bad, I panicked, thinking I would not reach him before surgery. I decided to call one of our partners, Buddy, in case he would see or speak to Cliff before I did.

"Buddy, it's Alesia."

"Hey, how are you feeling? I spoke to Cliff earlier, and he said he was picking you up. The weather is really bad so give him extra time to come get you, okay? We all look forward to seeing you soon."

I became hysterical and could barely speak but managed to tell Buddy what was happening and why I had called.

"I need to find Cliff to tell him they are taking me to surgery again

135

within the next hour," I cried. "I cannot let them take me without seeing him. I have no way to reach him on the road, and I don't know what to do. If you speak to him between, please let him know."

Although he really did not know me, Buddy was sincere and reassured me that everything was going to be okay.

At 6:00 p.m., the nurses began my new IV's and were putting me on the gurney to transport me to surgery. The nurses promised to fill my husband in when he arrived, but I was still unhappy about what was happening. I wondered if the doctors were not telling me everything and if the rush to surgery had something to do with it. I was letting my mind take over and imagining that things were worse than they explained.

As I was about to climb onto the gurney, Cliff appeared in the doorway. He looked quite puzzled, standing there with a bag of warm clothing, my jacket, and a big pair of snow boots.

"Seems as if we won't need these," he said as he walked toward me. "What's going on?"

I explained to him what was going on and how hard I had tried to get in touch with him, only to keep missing him along the way. As Cliff digested what was happening, the surgical staff wheeled me to my second surgery in ten days. He followed the gurney as far as he could before being taken to a small waiting room. I had told him the doctors felt that it would be a short surgery, so he would not have to wait too long to see me again.

Days later, Cliff told me the story of what actually happened. After about three hours in the room, he began to panic and think that he was forgotten or in the wrong room. He went back to the floor where my room was to speak to the nurses, who were puzzled to see him. Thinking that since so many hours had passed, I was surely in recovery. They made some calls and could not get any information. All they could tell him—over four hours later—was that I was still in surgery. Puzzled, he stayed put so the nurses could keep him posted. He tried to stay calm.

After another two hours slowly passed, he began to panic again. "It has been six hours since they took her to surgery," he said to the head nurse, trying to keep his cool. "Has something terrible happened and you are just unable to tell me?" At that point, he assumed the worst: that maybe I had died and they were not telling him.

Indeed, things had not gone well in the operating room. They woke me up at the end of surgery. My eyes were very heavy, but I struggled to open them and slowly looked around the room. There were a dozen people in the operating room, all busy doing things. I tried to speak but nothing came out. The nurse leaned over me to hear what I had to say.

"I can't feel my arm," I whispered to her.

"What did you say?" she asked. Everything—her voice, the movement in the room—sounded very loud to me.

"I can't feel my arm," I told her again.

Another nurse came over, and together they moved my right arm.

"I can't feel it," I repeated.

"She is kind of young to have had a stroke," one of them said to the other as they called more nurses over to look.

I wanted to cry, but no tears would come. Hoarse from the anesthesia, I could barely whisper as I tried to answer their questions. I fell asleep again, but awoke briefly to feel the gurney being moved. Someone was walking alongside the bed, speaking to me.

"Alesia, we are taking you to intensive care for the night. Your right side has suffered a trauma, and we need to monitor you. All you need to do is rest. We will bring your husband to you for a few minutes."

Too drugged to understand what they were saying, I simply nodded. "Am I going to be alright?" I whispered.

"Yes, but we are taking you to intensive care just to make sure," someone answered.

In the room, I opened my eyes again and saw Cliff. "What is happening?" I asked. He looked worried but told me he thought I would be fine. "Rest, and I will be back tomorrow." He explained that it was way after midnight and assured me he would be back in the morning. "I love you," I heard him say, then felt him kiss my forehead before I fell asleep.

I awoke, thinking it was morning and saw a nurse moving around the bed. I was groggy but more alert than the night before. "What is happening? Why am I here? Why can't I move my right arm?"

"The doctor will be in very soon. Go back to sleep until he arrives." Next thing I knew, Dr. Rosenberg was looking down at me and asking how I felt.

"I can't move my arm, and I'm not sure what is going on," I continued.

"When we got you to surgery, we assumed you had a little scar tissue to eliminate, and we would be in and out within an hour. What happened surprised and shocked us and also concerned us. You had just had surgery ten days ago, so it seemed very strange the amount of scar tissue that grew. You were in surgery for over five hours with two teams working on you. Scar tissue had overpowered your intestinal tract and we sent samples out to be tested. We have also discovered from patients who had surgery years ago that the powder from the surgical gloves sometimes came off inside of them, causing allergic reactions. This may have happened to you. We sent out samples to check for powder residue and are awaiting results."

He continued. "As for the arm, we are sending a specialist in to take a look at you. We think that when we strapped your arm on the operating table, it was turned very slightly. From the amount of time you were in surgery, your arm being in that position may have resulted in some nerve damage. People generally regain full movement, but we need to have you checked out to assure us that it is nothing more serious. We also placed a tube inside your intestinal tract to keep everything in place. It begins in your nose and runs through about 25 feet of your intestines to hold everything still."

Twenty-five feet!? I thought. It sounded like ten miles to me. How could I have 25 feet of anything placed inside my body?

"If you grow more scar tissue, we think it will grow around this tube. After some time, we will remove the tube and it will loosen the scar tissue, therefore not choking your intestines. They should remain in place when the tube is removed."

"What do you mean 'people generally regain full movement'? How often does the arm not recover? What am I going to do in the mean time? I have almost no movement. I can't even hold anything. And how is that tube coming out? How far down is it?" I asked, realizing I had two tubes, one in each nostril.

It may have seemed strange that I was asking such questions under sedation, but I had been through just about every procedure having to do with my stomach and intestinal tract, so I knew what to ask, and I wanted answers to everything. Dr. Rosenberg was informative and reassuring.

"Let's wait and see," he explained. "We will keep you here a few days and then get you into a regular room."

Later that day, still heavily sedated and in intensive care, a doctor came to examine my arm and test my motor skills and memory skills. Cliff was there and was as confused as I was about what had happened. This new doctor told us that the nerve damage in my arm would heal with therapy, that all movement and sensation should come back. He also informed us that my short-term memory may have been affected, but it would return to normal, as well. Uncertain what to ask him, we just listened.

After a few days, they sent me to a regular room where I could watch television to pass the time and have company to cheer me up. I was taken to a floor where everyone was actually up and around on crutches. I realized this was a first for me—on a floor where everyone wasn't plugged in, hooked up, stuck in bed, and extremely ill.

"Where am I?" I asked, still drugged. In fact, I was still hooked up to a pain pump that allowed me to administer my own doses of pain medication at ten-minute intervals. They had moved me to a new bed with all of my machines and wires.

"We were short on beds so we brought you to this floor temporarily. These patients are recovering from limb surgery. Most are headed home after a few days," a nurse told me. What I did not know until later that night was that the nurses on this floor were not surgically able to take care of a patient like me. I was happy to be in a room but woke up a few hours later to find the nurse sitting by the bed reading the directions on the pain medication machine. I was scared to death. It was the middle of the night, and I was alone with a nurse who didn't know what she was doing. She explained that she was struggling to get the machine to work, and I dozed off, only to wake up a short time later in terrible pain. She was still sitting there, playing with the machine. Too terrified to go back to sleep, I lay there watching the clock as the minutes crept by.

Dr. Rosenberg came in early and asked how I was. When I explained how my night went, he began to make calls. "Why would we move a patient from intensive care if we had no beds for her in the proper setting!?" He yelled into the phone. He had me moved immediately to a surgical floor with the hospital's apologies. I was so relieved that I went right to sleep and had an uneventful night.

I had a long road to recovery, and that's exactly what I focused on: recovery. Meanwhile, my parents took care of Johnathan for twelve days. One day, Cliff called and said he had spoken with my father. My mom had developed a bad case of shingles and had to be sedated. Dad was unsure if she could care for my son anymore.

Cliff said he would go get Johnathan and work out something with a sitter for him. "I'll put him in daycare during the day so I can work, and then bring him home nights to care for him. I may not be able to get to see you as much, but we'll work it out."

Realizing there was nothing I could do but let go and trust my husband, I agreed. "Well, I guess you're going to have to figure it out since we don't know when I can come home. He will adjust to whatever you do, and he will be fine. He has no choice, just like me."

Cliff continued to come visit when someone would babysit at night, sitting by my bed and telling me about his day. He shuffled between home and clubs, caring for Johnathan and the dogs, and driving the hour to see me when he could. Although I felt bad for him, I felt sorrier for myself—completely helpless with no end in sight.

Days became weeks and I was beginning to show improvement, but since my surgeries had been so close together it was taking twice as long to get me back on my feet. I cried every day, missing my baby, but when my father did bring him, within minutes I needed them to take him home. He wanted to climb into bed and lay with me. I was in so much pain, anyone just touching my bed, causing any movement, made me cry out. Since I couldn't hold him, Johnathan wanted to run around the halls; normal for a 2-year old, so we kept his visits short and sweet. He even told me I looked like Snuffalupagous from Sesame Street, the brown elephant with the long nose. The tubes in both of my nostrils must have looked similar to him and he even tried to draw a picture for me of the character. It made me laugh; at least I didn't scare him.

Many x-rays later, it seemed as if my intestinal tract was healing very slowly, and I could not take in liquids by mouth without becoming ill. I was so thirsty always but could only take about one ounce at a time, over three hour periods in order not to have it come back up. I wasn't too happy about this, but tried to make the best of it by having the nurses freeze juices and/or have my friends bring me flavored ice so that I could eat slowly and feel the cold liquid in my throat.

After five weeks, the doctors let me try soft foods. It was difficult to eat anything with two tubes still hanging out of my nose. It felt good to actually eat food again, but after not eating for so long, a couple spoonfuls of soup or pudding filled me up. Gradually, I was weaned to regular foods, and it was finally time to remove the tubes.

The NG tube was first to go. "Okay, relax and when I count to three, we will pull. It will be over in a second," Dr. Horowitz said in a reassuring tone. I knew the drill from years before, but I was uptight every time. "One, two, three," he counted…and before I knew it, I was one tube short. Gagging and coughing, but with one less tube. "We will remove the other one in a few days," he explained.

"Will you sedate me?" I asked.

"No, you will be fine," he said.

"Twenty five feet down sounds pretty deep to me, and I would be much happier to be knocked out." The thought of 25 feet of tubing running through my body had haunted me for weeks, and the thought of them pulling it all out through my nose without sedation horrified me. I literally felt ill at the thought of it.

"Let's wait and see when the time comes," was his answer.

Friday came and both of my surgeons were off for the weekend. An associate came to the room and asked if I was ready to have the last tube taken out. I hesitated and told him I preferred to be knocked out.

"We do not need to do that, but if you are afraid, I will have the nurse give you some Valium. That will relax you enough," he said.

After the Valium was administered, the doctor came back to see me very relaxed but still scared. He untaped my nose from where the tube was held into place and told me that he would pull on the count of three. I was nervous, having spent the last 5 ½ weeks thinking about this tube and how far down it was. On "three," he started to pull the tube, but I grabbed it so tight he could not get it out.

"I am not letting you do this!" I cried out. "I am too scared! I wanna be put out for this!"

He began to argue with me but I refused to remove my hands from the tube. I began to feel sick to my stomach. "You need to let go and let me do my job," he said.

"No, knock me out! Please knock me out!"

He told the nurse to keep giving me the Valium and said that he would be back over the weekend. I am not sure if it was the small jolt of the tube or my nerves, but I spent the rest of the weekend vomiting and sleeping. On Monday, I would not let him near me and was obviously upset when Dr. Rosenberg got to the room.

"What's happening?" he asked when he saw me.

I was physically shaken, crying, and very sick. "I told your associate to knock me out, put me in twilight, to remove this tube because I was so afraid and he refused. I wouldn't let him touch me or the tube. I spent the weekend like this."

"I cannot believe he left you like this," he went on. "I will talk with him, but in the meantime, let's get this out of you."

Within the hour, I was half knocked out and wheeled into a small room. The next thing I knew, my hand was over my nose with a gauze pad, and I was asking them when they were going to begin.

"It's over, out, done," Dr. Rosenberg said. "You are a free woman, and in a few days, you should be able to go home."

"That's it?" I asked, shocked that it went so quickly. I realized in my hazy state that despite all of the surgeries I had been through in my life, dealing with that tube was the most horrifying thing I had experienced.

Later in the evening when Cliff came to see me, he was pleased and surprised. With the exception of the IV, I was tube-free, moving around slowly, and more independent than I had been in six weeks.

Six weeks after the drama began, it was time to go home. After weeks of therapy, the strength in my arm began to improve, and my memory began to come back. Dr. Rosenberg told me it would take a long time to recover completely but to take it slowly. The test for powder from the surgical gloves did not show any residue in my system, meaning that the scar tissue had grown rapidly enough to cause the problem. "All we can do is pray it never happens again," the doctor told me. "Good luck and take your time recovering."

Coming home was an adjustment for all of us. I was unable to lift anything, even my child, or do anything strenuous for 3 months. I taught Johnathan to climb onto the couch and very gently climb into my lap, even when he was crying, so I could hold him. When he was in my lap, he was not allowed to kick or move a lot for fear he would hurt me. He learned this quickly and had no choice but to follow the rules. I also taught him to hand me things that were on the floor, and not to be rough while he was playing. My right arm was still very weak and holding anything in my hands was difficult, as well.

I visited the specialist about my arm and my memory, but both problems eventually went away. We were thankful it had not been a stroke and that all movement came back. I don't recall how long it took to completely recover, but I wasn't able to lift Johnathan for months.

I chalked this up as another experience in life and moved on. I later had nightmares about all that I had experienced during those 6 ½ weeks in the hospital, and I worried every time I had a pain that it might be happening again.

Chapter 37

MY MOTHER

My mother was a wonderful person and friend,
and losing her left me questioning many things.

My mother was a wonderful person and friend, and losing her left me questioning many things. I healed over the years, however, and understand more deeply about life and death. Mom was there for me through everything in my life, including the birth of my only child. She and Dad would do anything for me, my siblings, and our extended families.

Mom's name was Evelyn. She developed a rare disease of the brain called Church Hill Syndrome, or vasculitis, and Dad cared for her for six years before she finally passed away. Her disease attacked parts of the brain and the signals were sent throughout her body, sometimes signaling false problems and other times very real and serious illnesses. Dad took wonderful care of her and pushed her to do things she was unable to do without his help and encouragement.

Cliff and I believe that Johnathan played a major role in her will to live. Her relationship with Johnathan from birth was so special for them both and left him with a wonderful memory of his grandmother. Even so, it saddens me that she will not see him graduate high school or college or get married.

While she was still with us, we made every effort to spend as much time with her as possible. "Mom, Cliff and I are canceling our vacation to be near you because you've been in the hospital for so long," I told her one day when Johnathan and I went to visit. Even Johnathan wanted to stay with his "Me-mom," a nickname he came up with on his own. He was 5 years old at the time, and my health had been steadily improving since surgery.

"Don't be ridiculous," she said. "Go, have fun, and when you get back, maybe I will be home."

Against my better judgment, we drove to Florida with Johnathan. As soon as we arrived, my father called me. "Mom has passed," he said.

"She waited for me to leave because she did not want me to push her to keep going," I told Cliff. I felt terrible for my father and my sister, having to handle things while I prepared to head back home.

My brother and his family lived in Florida—and still do—and we all gathered to make a plan for traveling.

Cliff was concerned, "You are not in any condition to drive home yet, and we'll need to wait a few days for you to be able to make the trip back and care for Johnathan." We all agreed to wait and put things in order before going back. Within a week, we were there preparing for mom's funeral.

I remember the funeral as if were yesterday. It was the worst day of my life. We decided to leave Johnathan home because he was so very young—I could not bring myself to tell him she had died or to let him see her in a casket.

It was about 20 degrees the morning of the service, and the ride was solemn from New Jersey to Philadelphia. Everyone I was close to was already at the grave when we arrived. It began to snow lightly, and we all huddled together to listen to the rabbi and to the prayers for Mom. I trembled so hard Cliff had to hold onto me so I would not chatter. The wind whipped, and the snow continued to fall, as did the tears. I was numb, unable to accept the fact that my best friend was gone, and I felt very alone even though all those who loved me were present. *Mom, what will I do without you?* I screamed silently. *Who will be there for me when I need to talk? How can I go on?*

Dad took us all out to eat in lieu of going back to someone's home. According to Jewish culture, 3–7 days after burial is called Shiva, and all who want to visit are welcome to come to the home and pay respects. Dad could not handle the stress and wanted to just come to my home and "sit Shiva" alone. He told Cliff and me, "I sat Shiva for the past 6 years caring for mom.

She was sick almost constantly, and I need to free myself from the sadness I have experienced."

We understood, even though it was very untraditional.

Despite my own sadness, I went to the gym early the following morning. I felt I had two choices in my life: to stay at home for a long time—which is what I really wanted to do—and eat myself into obesity, or to immediately do something good for myself and make myself strong for me and for my family. Dad was waiting for me when I got back later that morning, and he, Cliff, and I spent the following few days sitting Shiva. Dad got to enjoy his grandson and help him understand what had happened to his Me-Mom.

I became brave enough to tell Johnathan the truth a few days after the funeral. "Me-mom has gone to heaven because she has been so sick, but she will be happier there. She now looks down upon us every moment to make sure we are all okay."

Johnathan seemed to reflect for a moment and said, "Mom, can Me-mom see me always and will she see us all forever?"

"Yes," I assured him. "Me-mom can see us always and at night, I want you to look into the sky and look for the brightest star. When you find it, wave and smile, because that is your Me-mom shining on you."

He looked at me again for a moment with his big green eyes and smiled. He was satisfied with what he had been told. To this day, he has a picture of his Me-mom holding him at about 4 years old. It is one of the few my mother allowed to be taken of her, and I see it when I enter his bedroom every day.

CHAPTER 38

MY CHILDREN

*Kerry took to Johnathan from the moment he was born,
even though she was only 17 years old at the time.*

I became very close to Cliff's daughter Kerry because she spent every other weekend with us from the time she was seven. She always treated me as if I was one of her parents, and I included her in as much of my pregnancy as I could. I even had Cliff bring her with us for an ultrasound so she could see the baby and hear his heartbeat. I wanted her to feel like this was a full sibling and that she could love him and see him any time she chose. As a result, they became extremely close.

Kerry took to Johnathan from the moment he was born, even though she was only 17 years old at the time. When he was very young, she promised to call him often. Like every young person, however, life got in the way and the calls were infrequent—but his loyalty to her never faltered. He talked about her often and patiently waited for her to return to him, often bragging about her to his friends. He spoke of her as if he saw her every day and could not wait to introduce his little friends to his "sister."

Johnathan went to Kerry's one time while she still lived with her mother. He came home and asked me, "Mom, since you are Kerry's step mom, then that means that Kerry's mom is my step mom, right?"

"Well, that is not so Johnathan, because daddy was married to both of us so that is why that makes me Kerry's half mom. You are not related to Kerry's mom."

"I want her to be my step mom," he cried. "If Kerry has a step mom, then

I want one, too." He was very indignant.

All I could do was smile and tell him, "I am sure that if you asked Kerry's mom, she would be happy to be your step mom. She would love to have a little boy like you." He seemed satisfied, and I think he even asked her at some point and the answer was yes.

Johnathan also asked my neighbor's mother to be his step grandma. He loved her so much before my mother passed; she was the really cool grandma that all the neighborhood kids liked. When Me-mom passed away, he marched right up to the neighbor and asked, "Nan, would you be my grandma now?" She reached for him, hugged him, and said, "Of course, Johnathan, I would love to be your grandma now." He seemed satisfied with his growing family.

By the time she was in her late 20s, Kerry was dating a wonderful guy. When she and Mike decided to get married, you would have thought that Johnathan was marrying him as well because of his obvious love for Mike. A few years and two kids later, Johnathan became an uncle.

Johnathan visits Kerry and Mike on his own now, which confirms that their relationship is a special one and will be strong forever. He is such a young uncle that his nieces will always look up to him just like he looked up to his older sister.

CHAPTER 39

ANOTHER BUSINESS?

*The prior owner was aging and not interested in keeping things up,
whereas we were young, ambitious, and crazy enough to take on
the project, which I called the "money pit."*

In 1996, not long after my mom passed, Cliff decided he wanted to buy his
favorite restaurant. Within eight months, the Sweetwater Casino Restaurant and Marina was ours. Despite its name, there was no gambling. The
place was probably about 80 years old when we got it, and rumor said that
it had probably been a speakeasy and poker haven back in the day. It was in
a beautiful setting along the Mullica River, but it had been failing for a few
years. Located in the small town of Sweetwater, New Jersey, the property
included twelve acres, most of them located along the river. The restaurant
seated about 250 for inside dining, and another 100 on an outside deck.
There was also an inside bar and lounge, a marina for 80 boat slips, and a full
gift shop. This property was in the Pine Barrens, protected by Pinelands,
which meant getting permits for building, expanding, or growing in or
around the area was extremely difficult.

Every night, watching the sun set behind beautiful pine trees across the
river, I would mention to the customers, "Because Pinelands protects this
perfect view, the sun will always set behind those trees. It's perfect, and it's
one of the reasons we bought this place."

The prior owner was aging and not interested in keeping things up,
whereas we were young, ambitious, and crazy enough to take on the project,
which I called the "money pit." We took on two other partners and I went

back to work when our son was six. We renovated the entire property: landscaping, constructing a new kitchen, and completely remodeling. We put our heart and soul into it to make it a great success. The first five years were growth, but the second five we were bursting at the seams. Of course, this came with a high price. Our son practically grew up there, which was not a bad thing, but it became very consuming to me. We employed 40-60 people depending on the time of year and the restaurant sat hundreds of guests. I learned very quickly, that even though we had managers, we had to watch every little thing and know what was going on or we could lose it all. We caught one manager stealing, another one grew tired after a few years, and we had to buy out one of the partners within the first year of operation.

Being in the restaurant business was like being married. Everyone who worked for us was family: we employed some real characters and were frequented by others.

One customer was extremely intelligent but his alcohol intake was so extreme and his conversation so annoying that we banned him from entering. Another guy, whom everyone called Captain Norm, was also an alcoholic. He insulted people, stole bartender's tips off the bar, and pestered anyone who sat down. Captain Norm was also banned.

Among the comical people who worked for us were a waitress who wore no undies and lifted up her skirt in the kitchen to show the cooks, and another employee who told everyone that he was an undercover sharpshooter for the CIA.

"Cliff, even though I know that guy's family, he spooks me when he talks about the CIA and killing people, even those he works with," I said one day. "Time to lay him off so he doesn't threaten anyone else. We will let him go gracefully, so that he is not threatened." We told him we just weren't busy enough to keep him, and he said he had an undercover mission to take care of anyway. Everybody parted happily.

One night a server dropped a flaming pepper steak, which managed to flip up in the air and—still flaming—land right on the plate that fell upright on the floor. He then proceeded to pick up the plate and serve the steak right off the floor.

There was an argument in the kitchen one night while I was trying to help. The 120-degree heat near the ovens combined with the 90-degree outside summertime temperature had everyone edgy. Two cooks got mad at each other while we were really busy. In a split second, one picked up a prime rib and threw it at the other cook two places down on the cook line. The guy in the middle ducked and never looked up or stopped what he was doing. I was mad but almost laughed out loud at the scene, which looked like a skit from Saturday Night Live. We were too busy to deal with them at the time it happened, but they were both reprimanded when we were done for the evening.

If I hadn't laughed, I would have cried—something I did periodically toward the end of the ten years we were there. But I also remember the wonderful Christmas parties we threw for our staff and the Christmas stories I wrote about everyone so that they could laugh at themselves and remember how much fun they had. Over the years, we heard things from past employees like, "You were the best bosses I ever had."

It always felt good to hear those things, as we were good, fair, and honest employers.

CHAPTER 40

PHILANTHROPY

We still support the research center and keep up with all of the new and upcoming research involving HIV and AIDS.

Giving back was nothing new to us. We began in both of our nightclubs in the early 1980s when we read that Dr. Steven Douglas at The Children's Hospital of Philadelphia was beginning research on pediatric AIDS. Because of my long connection with the hospital, Cliff and I felt it would be a great opportunity to give back and to help raise money and awareness for the "new disease" that was killing our friends. Once a year, we had both clubs redecorated for a night, and we arranged for celebrities, fashion shows, and casino entertainment to come and donate their time. We minimized our expenses, which allowed us to give nearly all of the money raised to the hospital. Dr. Douglas was thrilled with this new way of creating awareness and helping his research blossom into an entire department. We still support the research center and keep up with all of the new and upcoming research involving HIV and AIDS.

Buying the restaurant was a major endeavor for us since we had a young child and two other businesses. One of my motivating factors was the community, family-oriented atmosphere we could inspire. With so much successful fundraising under our belts in our nightclubs, it excited us to think what we could do at the restaurant. With Sweetwater being a small town and Mullica being one of the smallest townships in South Jersey, we wanted to involve everyone in a community fundraiser.

One of our good customers had a sick grandchild named Timmy, and the family needed financial help. Planning a big event would help the boy and his family and, hopefully, bring the community together.

We quickly organized a meeting with the boy's family, our managers, and some friends. Only a few people from the community showed up, but we knew we were onto something good. "Let's do something on the water since it is so beautiful here in the summertime," Cliff suggested.

"A boat parade would be nice," I agreed, "but how can we raise money for Timmy's family?"

"How about a kids' carnival?" said Joyce, our manager at the time.

One of Timmy's aunts thought we could get prizes for the kids, have games, and have t-shirts made for the event.

"Let's have a boat parade in the evening and give out prizes…and have a motorcycle run in the morning," someone else suggested.

We were off and running. With meetings every two weeks from there on out, we soon had a full blown committee and named the foundation Timmy's Regatta. About 1,500 people showed up and donated in various ways. Money came in through sponsorships, carnival ticket sales, food sales, and fees for the motorcycle run and boat parade. All told, we raised about $25,000 for the family. Timmy recovered fully from the tumor that once threatened to take his life, and he is now in his 20s and doing well.

With every passing year, Timmy's Regatta picked up momentum. It became so big that after the first three years, the gifts donated for us to give away were substantial, such as trips, jewelry, and valuable crystals. Our opening meeting one season included new ideas on how to handle these prizes. We decided to include a live auction the evening before with no admission charge and complimentary champagne and hors d'ouevres. This would add to the final total of the event and make the entire experience a charity weekend. Many prominent business people from our area attended, and we raised close to $25,000 in one evening.

Timmy's Regatta began by helping one child and his family, but it developed into a major community outreach. Over the ten years that we owned the restaurant, it helped 10 families with sick family members. Thousands of people came from 30–90 miles away just to donate money and be a part of our great outreach. One year, we managed to raise about $80,000 for a family.

One of the most rewarding moments at our regatta was when my son Johnathan, then about 10 years old, put a dollar in a raffle for a brand new boy's bike and won. In the middle of the day, surrounded by thousands of people, I looked up and heard the announcement of the bicycle winner. At first I was uncertain as to why his name was being announced, then I realized he won the bike. He came running over to me with a big smile and out of breath to tell me what had happened. My initial reaction to him did not go over too well.

"Johnathan," I said softly, "you cannot keep the bike. It is not fair to the other children here, and you should give it back for someone less fortunate to have."

He began to cry and said, "It's my bike, I won it and I am not giving it back!" All I could think of was that someone would say the drawing was fixed.

A customer who overheard us talking stepped in to give his opinion. "Let your son keep the bike. He won it and should be allowed to keep it."

I thought for a moment, looked at Johnathan and decided to give in. He really did win fair and square and was bubbling over with excitement. "Okay," I told him, "it's yours." No one ever said a word to me. I guess they trusted that we were fair to everyone and tried to have all the kids there leave the carnival with some kind of prize, even my own kid.

Organizing and running the regatta was probably one of the most rewarding things I have done in my life. My own experiences as a sick child put other people's illnesses into perspective for me and, by extension, for so many others. Helping people seems to complete everything else I have done with my life, and it is the reason I wake up every day. The planning and hard work, watching the plans unfold, and looking into the faces of the people we helped fills me with a sense of warmth.

After ten years, we decided to sell our restaurant and had our last regatta in 2005. The restaurant burned down in June 2008 and has not been rebuilt. All of our hard work, dreams, and picture collections went up in smoke, leaving us only memories of the hard work and great success. I cried as I approached the charred remains when we sold the property—the magic burned down with that place.

CHAPTER 41

HERE WE GO
AGAIN AND AGAIN

⟿

"This could be the chance of a lifetime. I cannot pass up this opportunity,
and at this stage of my life, I think I have one last major project in
me..." my crazy husband said to me.

The phone rang one day, and I picked it up. "I got a great deal for you to check out on your next trip to Florida," Buddy, our partner in Atlantic City, said. "Hard Rock is going to open a hotel casino on the Seminole Indian Reservation in Hollywood, Florida. They are already building, and they want us to open a nightclub there with them," he continued. *Oh boy*, I thought, and handed the phone directly to Cliff.

"I will take a look when we go down there," was Cliff's calm, cool reaction.

"Are you crazy?" I asked him. "We have two nightclubs and a restaurant, and I am half crazy as it is. You must have lost it," I said.

"This could be the chance of a lifetime. I cannot pass up this opportunity, and at this stage of my life, I think I have one last major project in me. I'm taking a look at the situation to see if we can swing it," my crazy husband said to me.

He and Buddy went to Florida and learned that the Hard Rock would be the only gaming casino with a major hotel associated with it. When the two of them returned, they had made a deal.

"All we have to do is liquidate some of our other business interests, and then we can move to Florida," Cliff told me.

155

For a few years, Cliff was traveling weekly to Florida to work on construction and planning, and I juggled home, work, and our teenage son. Things were getting more difficult at our restaurant; the stress of working and having a child was wearing on me. On top of that, two years had passed, and we still hadn't sold our interests in the other businesses. Easier said than done, indeed.

The Hard Rock Hotel and Casino was scheduled to open, and we were involved in the next phase, which was building the nightclubs and restaurants. Meantime, the hotel had us operating a temporary nightclub inside the casino.

This was a major undertaking, and I went to visit the site for the first time. The project had been in the first phase for a couple of years, and our nightclub wouldn't be built for another 8 months or so. Cliff and I flew down to Hollywood, checked into a hotel nearby, and went to the site. We pulled onto the Seminole Reservation, and I was surprised by the beautiful sprawling gardens and buildings. The hotel stood out above everything else around it, and I was instantly impressed with all that I saw when I stepped out of the car. Everything about the building was perfect: the floors, walls, style, and color. The employees greeted us warmly, and we went to the temporary ballroom that would serve as our nightclub until construction was complete.

While Cliff was busy with orchestrating how the first night would unfold, I wandered around with our partner's wife Helene, who had also come down for the opening. We found the pool area, which was an amazing four acres of tropical paradise, including its own beach and waterfalls. We wandered into the back hallways and found all the ballrooms, then looked for where the next building phase would be so we could check out our nightclub site. We made it outside to the construction site—a "hardhat area only"—but no one stopped us. The entire complex was utterly foolproof; they had thought of everything.

Helene and I had an almost immediate change of heart about our next business venture. We were both on board! Selling everything and moving to the warm climate suddenly seemed like something we could do, and we agreed that maybe this was not such a bad idea after all.

Cliff and I dined with Buddy and Helene that night and toasted the opening of our newest business. After dinner, we headed to our temporary home in the casino. When we opened the doors—using staff we had brought from home in New Jersey—we became an instant success. The night was perfect, and customers were anxious for us to move into our permanent home outside the building. We left Florida that weekend with big dreams of our future and an excitement neither of us had felt since we bought the restaurant.

"The complex is beautiful," I told Cliff on the way home, admitting, "I am glad you did not listen to me. This is the opportunity of a lifetime and it would have been wrong not to be involved."

We finally got some bites on our businesses and at one point I told Cliff, "We need to sell, if not for anything other than our health." The two of us were separated too much, I was too busy to travel with him most of the time, and our son had too much freedom when I did go. One by one, each business went, and in a year's time, the only thing we owned in New Jersey was our home. Finally, we could put some thought into the rest of our lives.

After careful consideration, we decided not to move and uproot our son, who was then in the middle of high school, and agreed we would allow him to graduate with his friends and then decide where we wanted to go.

For now, Cliff travels often but has cut his schedule down to spend time with his family. I have decided to focus on my writing career so I can be home for my husband and son, and life has reached some sort of calm. Family comes first, and time together is the most important thing. Only time will tell what will happen in the future, and I live by the saying, "good things come to those who wait."

CHAPTER 42

FINAL REFLECTION

*I have a positive attitude toward life
and believe that everything happens for a reason.*

Through the years, I have learned more about people in the bar business than any psychology class could have ever taught me. I can read people in a split second, and I am 99% right 99% of the time. People have auras, and I learned to read them even when I don't mean to. When people drink alcohol, they also let their guards down and tell you things they would never normally talk about. Needless to say, I've had lots of opportunities to talk with people in that state.

I have been through so much—both mentally and physically—in my life, and I use that inner strength to guide me in all of my decisions, even when they aren't the best ones or the correct ones. My childhood molded me into a strong teenager, and that continued into my adulthood. My ability to speak up when something does not sit right must be partly from the amount of therapy I went through in the two years prior to surgery. Week after week of sitting with a therapist taught me to think before I speak, to try to be logical, and to look at the big picture before making a final decision.

I believe there is always something better waiting for me. I have a positive attitude toward life and believe that everything happens for a reason. In addition to my parents, I have to thank Dr. Koop, Dr. Templeton, and my closest childhood friend Randee. My family and strong friendships have led me to believe that most people are good. I have learned to be discerning—not gullible.

I am happy to help those in need just as I have been helped. My husband believes in me and has always either helped or stood by with full support. Together we have learned to fundraise, give to those less fortunate, and to try to be there for anyone who has asked for our help. This has been extremely rewarding for both of us. In return, we have only asked for appreciation and nothing else.

I hope that this book helps heal some of you just as writing it has helped me heal. It has been both rewarding and challenging. For those that have taken this journey with me, I thank you.

Breinigsville, PA USA
17 September 2010
245585BV00001B/3/P

ABOUT THE AUTHOR

Alesia Shute was born in Philadelphia from a hard working family, and grew up in the Northeast with a dad who worked two jobs and a mom who stayed home with the kids. Alesia dreamed of being a fashion model most of her life, but her height kept her from fully following through. She thought about being a nurse, with her natural compassion for people, but her untimely illness at the age of 8 and subsequent six major surgeries, multiple minor surgeries and long hospital stays made her rethink that career.

In between all of her surgeries, Alesia met her husband, Cliff, whom she has been married to for 25 years. Together they have worked in the night-club and restaurant business for their entire relationship, balancing marriage and work; crazy-all-night, sleep-all-day work! She helped to raise his daughter, raise their son, and many, many dogs together. They now have two grandchildren from his daughter who give her more love than she could ask for.

Alesia is the proud recipient of the "Good Neighbor Award" for her work on fundraising for a local playground, and she and her husband are active donors to The Children's Hospital of Philadelphia. 'Pediatric Aids Research' is their favorite cause and together they have used their nightclubs as foundations to help raise money to aid the research department and its leading scientist Dr. Steven Douglas in increasing the size of the labs and pursuing many breakthroughs over the past 30 years in Aids Research.

They have used their businesses to hold carnivals and auctions to help families with sick children to pay the bills. Alesia was the president of the Timmy's Regatta Foundation for 10 years and She and Cliff still donate to Ronald McDonald House in Camden New Jersey, as well as to local charities that encourage neighborhood children to participate in sports.